W9-ABJ-551

Human Rights

Other Books of Related Interest:

At Issue Series

Is Torture Ever Justified?

Racial Profiling

Transgendered People

What Rights Should Illegal Immigrants Have?

Women in Islam

Global Viewpoints Series

Death and Dying

Women's Rights

Introducing Issues with Opposing Viewpoints Series

Animal Rights

Civil Liberties

Death and Dying

The Death Penalty

Gay Marriage

Issues That Concern You Series

Censorship

Opposing Viewpoints Series

Abortion

Gays in the Military

War Crimes

Social Issues in Literature

Colonialism in Chinua Achebe's *Things Fall Apart*

Freedom of Thought in Jerome Lawrence & Robert Edwin Lee's *Inherit the Wind*

GLOBALVIEWPOINTS

Human Rights

Margaret Haerens, Book Editor

GREENHAVEN PRESS
A part of Gale, Cengage Learning

GALE
CENGAGE Learning

Detroit • New York • San Francisco • New Haven, Conn • Waterville, Maine • London

Christine Nasso, *Publisher*
Elizabeth Des Chenes, *Managing Editor*

© 2011 Greenhaven Press, a part of Gale, Cengage Learning

Gale and Greenhaven Press are registered trademarks used herein under license.

For more information, contact:
Greenhaven Press
27500 Drake Rd.
Farmington Hills, MI 48331-3535
Or you can visit our Internet site at gale.cengage.com

For product information and technology assistance, contact us at

Gale Customer Support, 1-800-877-4253
For permission to use material from this text or product, submit all requests online at www.cengage.com/permissions

Further permissions questions can be emailed to permissionrequest@cengage.com

Articles in Greenhaven Press anthologies are often edited for length to meet page requirements. In addition, original titles of these works are changed to clearly present the main thesis and to explicitly indicate the author's opinion. Every effort is made to ensure that Greenhaven Press accurately reflects the original intent of the authors. Every effort has been made to trace the owners of copyrighted material.

Cover image © Steve Turner/Alamy.

LIBRARY OF CONGRESS CATALOGING-IN-PUBLICATION DATA

Human rights / Margaret Haerens, book editor.
    p. cm. -- (Global viewpoints)
    Includes bibliographical references and index.
    ISBN 978-0-7377-5193-2 (hardcover) -- ISBN 978-0-7377-5194-9 (pbk.)
    1. Human rights. I. Haerens, Margaret.
    JC571.H25 2011
    323--dc22
                                                            2010050622

Printed in the United States of America
1 2 3 4 5 6 7 15 14 13 12 11

Contents

Chapter 1: The Global State of Human Rights

Chapter 2: Human Rights and Politics

The military regime governing Myanmar has systematically oppressed political opposition through restrictive election laws, imprisonment of political dissidents and opponents, and violence. The Association of Southeast Asian Nations (ASEAN) must pressure Myanmar's government to finally hold fair elections and to respect the will of the people.

The European Union should continue its attempts to strengthen ties with the Central Asian countries of Turkmenistan and Uzbekistan in hopes of encouraging human rights reforms in both countries.

Chapter 3: Human Rights and Minority Populations

Estonia often ignores the widespread discrimination against ethnic Russians. A debate over how the Russians came to live in the region years ago is part of the friction.

Chapter 4: Human Rights Challenges

The International Criminal Court (ICC) is the only option for people in some African countries that lack a national initiative to prosecute war crimes, genocide, and other violations of human rights. The ICC must balance expectations and reality, and it must forge a practical approach to its basic mission.

Foreword

"The problems of all of humanity can only be solved by all of humanity."
—Swiss author Friedrich Dürrenmatt

Global interdependence has become an undeniable reality. Mass media and technology have increased worldwide access to information and created a society of global citizens. Understanding and navigating this global community is a challenge, requiring a high degree of information literacy and a new level of learning sophistication.

Building on the success of its flagship series, *Opposing Viewpoints*, Greenhaven Press has created the *Global Viewpoints* series to examine a broad range of current, often controversial topics of worldwide importance from a variety of international perspectives. Providing students and other readers with the information they need to explore global connections and think critically about worldwide implications, each *Global Viewpoints* volume offers a panoramic view of a topic of widespread significance.

Drugs, famine, immigration—a broad, international treatment is essential to do justice to social, environmental, health, and political issues such as these. Junior high, high school, and early college students, as well as general readers, can all use *Global Viewpoints* anthologies to discern the complexities relating to each issue. Readers will be able to examine unique national perspectives while, at the same time, appreciating the interconnectedness that global priorities bring to all nations and cultures.

Material in each volume is selected from a diverse range of sources, including journals, magazines, newspapers, nonfiction books, speeches, government documents, pamphlets, organization newsletters, and position papers. *Global Viewpoints* is truly global, with material drawn primarily from international sources available in English and secondarily from US sources with extensive international coverage.

Features of each volume in the *Global Viewpoints* series include:

- An **annotated table of contents** that provides a brief summary of each essay in the volume, including the name of the country or area covered in the essay.

- An **introduction** specific to the volume topic.

- A **world map** to help readers locate the countries or areas covered in the essays.

- For each viewpoint, an **introduction** that contains notes about the author and source of the viewpoint explains why material from the specific country is being presented, summarizes the main points of the viewpoint, and offers three **guided reading questions** to aid in understanding and comprehension.

- **For further discussion** questions that promote critical thinking by asking the reader to compare and contrast aspects of the viewpoints or draw conclusions about perspectives and arguments.

- A worldwide list of **organizations to contact** for readers seeking additional information.

- A **periodical bibliography** for each chapter and a **bibliography of books** on the volume topic to aid in further research.

- A comprehensive **subject index** to offer access to people, places, events, and subjects cited in the text, with the countries covered in the viewpoints highlighted.

Global Viewpoints is designed for a broad spectrum of readers who want to learn more about current events, history, political science, government, international relations, economics, environmental science, world cultures, and sociology—students doing research for class assignments or debates, teachers and faculty seeking to supplement course materials, and others wanting to understand current issues better. By presenting how people in various countries perceive the root causes, current consequences, and proposed solutions to worldwide challenges, *Global Viewpoints* volumes offer readers opportunities to enhance their global awareness and their knowledge of cultures worldwide.

Introduction

> *"The idea is a simple one—that freedom, justice, and peace for the world must begin with freedom, justice, and peace in the lives of individual human beings."*
>
> —Barack Obama,
> in his 2010 remarks
> to the UN General Assembly

On October 12, 2000, the USS *Cole*, a naval destroyer, was ordered to refuel in the Yemeni port of Aden. While it was moored, a small craft approached the destroyer and suddenly exploded, killing seventeen American soldiers. Thirty-nine others were hurt in the blast. The bombing had also ripped a large gash in the port side of the destroyer. It was the deadliest attack against a US naval vessel since 1987.

The attack also signaled the growing confidence and capabilities of the international terrorist organization al Qaeda, which would soon perpetrate the horrific attacks of September 11, 2001, on New York City and Washington, D.C. In June 2001, a video was released that featured Osama bin Laden taking responsibility for the USS *Cole* attack. It would be only a few months after the video was seen around the world that bin Laden and al Qaeda would achieve their biggest victory on American soil.

The bombing of the USS *Cole* also revealed to the world what Western intelligence agencies already knew: Yemen was a breeding ground for Islamic fundamentalists and often a safe harbor for al Qaeda and other terrorist groups. Much of that can be attributed to Yemen's turbulent history. One of the oldest centers of civilization in the Middle East, Yemen was once an essential port on the spice trade route in ancient times. In recent years, however, it has been torn apart by civil war and a vicious rebel movement in the north that displaced a quarter of a million people in 2009. The conflict between government forces and the rebels, known as the Houthis, got so heated that Saudi Arabian forces attacked the Houthis in late 2009.

Geography and topography were other factors in the spread of terrorism in Yemen. Bordered on the north by Saudi Arabia, al Qaeda operatives and other terrorist groups easily moved between the two countries, finding cover in isolated and sparsely populated mountainous regions. Coupled with the political unrest in many areas as well as a growing number of Islamic fundamentalists and terrorist sympathizers, the al Qaeda presence has remained a true and grave threat for the Yemeni government.

After the September 11, 2001, attacks on the United States, the Yemeni government decided to step up their efforts to eradicate that threat. Yemeni intelligence agencies and government troops began a concerted and concentrated effort to root out and detain suspected al Qaeda members and sympathizers. By November 2002, they had arrested and jailed more than a hundred suspects and provided intelligence information on hundreds more. In the following few years, numerous high-profile arrests of suspects and battles with al Qaeda members occurred, often resulting in death.

On December 25, 2009, Yemen's relationship to al Qaeda was catapulted back into the news when a young Nigerian man, Umar Farouk Abdulmutallab, unsuccessfully tried to blow up a Northwest Airlines airliner en route from Amsterdam to Detroit. During the subsequent investigation of the incident, it was revealed that Abdulmutallab had received terrorist training at an al Qaeda camp in Yemen. Once again, international pressure began to mount on the Yemeni government to ramp up its anti-terror campaign against al Qaeda and other Islamic fundamentalist terrorist groups. The United States, in particular, pledged to expand military and intelligence cooperation with Yemen. In early 2010 the Barack Obama administration announced a $155.3 million security assistance package for the country, with much of it earmarked for Yemen's Special Operation Forces to expand their counterterrorism operations.

In response, Yemen did step up its counterterrorism efforts by expanding cooperation with US intelligence agencies. In May 2010 it was reported that US military and intelligence agencies had significantly expanded their surveillance activities in Yemen, using reconnaissance aircraft to identify and track al Qaeda targets and providing valuable information to Yemeni intelligence and military forces.

Yemen's expanded and wide-ranging counterterrorism measures also spurred widespread criticism from human rights organizations. As the government's policies became more repressive and sweeping to catch al Qaeda members, it allegedly began turning to unlawful measures such as enforced disappearances, extrajudicial executions, arbitrary detention, violation of privacy, torture, and excessive use of force. Moreover, human rights organizations allege that those who report and speak out about the government's illegal and oppressive policies are targeted. Journalists, human rights activists, and lawyers have been jailed and tried by specialized courts created to prosecute terrorists and the media.

One such example of government overreach in Yemen is the siege of the *Al-Ayyam* newspaper in January 2010. The conflict between the government and the newspaper escalated when the government forcibly shut *Al-Ayyam* and seven other newspapers down on May 4, 2009, citing the papers' promotion of "separatism" and their concern for national unity. The tense situation exploded on May 13, 2009, when Yemeni security forces fired on the paper's offices. A month later, a leading journalist on the paper, Anis Ahmed Mansur Hamida, was sentenced to fourteen months in prison for "attacking national unity." A sit-in was organized to support the shuttered paper in January 2010. Once again, government security forces fired on the crowd, and a policeman and a security guard working for *Al-Ayyam* were killed. The siege lasted twenty-four hours, and several other people were injured during the shooting. A day later, the editor of the paper, Hisham Bashraheel, was arrested. He was put on trial in October for organizing an armed group and fomenting violence against the police.

Human rights groups cite this incident as just one in a series of attacks against the independent press in Yemen. Citing concerns about terrorism, or "national unity," newspapers are shut down, journalists are intimidated or abducted, and security forces are unleashed on protestors.

Instead of widespread condemnation for these human rights abuses, Yemen has been supported by countries in the West for its strong approach to fighting terrorism, particularly the threat of al Qaeda. Reported abuses and human rights violations have been overlooked, and aid as well as military and intelligence support continue to pour in for Yemeni forces.

With such success, the Yemeni government reportedly began using its expanded and sweeping counterterrorism powers against its perceived enemies: the Houthis in the north and other insurgents causing trouble in the south. By many accounts, these groups are not allied to al Qaeda but are local people dissatisfied with the government's policies against civilians. Human rights groups report that the Yemeni government overlooks this crucial distinction: They identify the homegrown rebels as terrorists, thereby unleashing a full range of unlawful, oppressive, and even fatal measures to combat the threat these groups pose—maintaining a cycle of injustice.

In Yemen and other countries, human rights organizations see a pattern of governments violating human rights to combat terrorism. In the following volume, two such examples are discussed: the Uighur (or Uyghur) population in China's Xinjiang province and the oppression of the Tamil people by the Sri Lankan government.

The authors of the viewpoints presented in *Global Viewpoints: Human Rights* discuss some of the key issues of worldwide concern: the global state of human rights, political aspects of the human rights issue, the treatment of minority populations, and the challenges that remain ahead. The information in this volume will provide insight into the significant challenges many countries face, particularly the struggle to establish national security while maintaining a strong human rights framework and the responsibility governments have to protect the human rights of all their people.

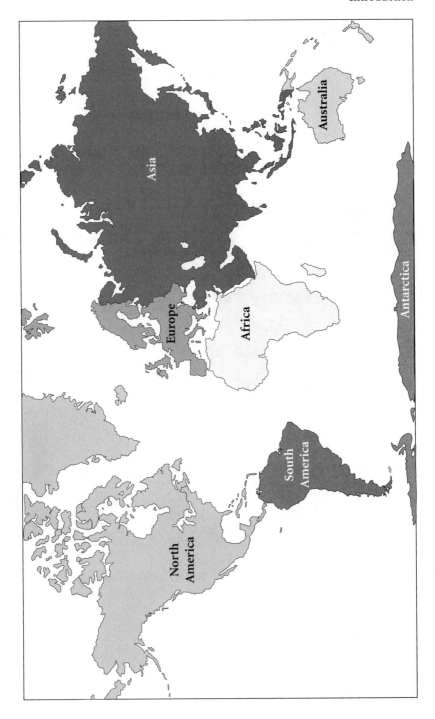

CHAPTER 1

The Global State of Human Rights

Global Human Rights: An Overview

Amnesty International

Amnesty International (AI) is an international nongovernmental organization that aims to address human rights abuses all over the world and advocate for the human rights of all people. In the following viewpoint, AI provides a summary of the recently released report on the global state of human rights, arguing that despite progress in many areas, a number of governments favored politics before justice.

As you read, consider the following questions:

1. Amnesty International's report documents abuses in how many countries?
2. How did the African Union respond to the International Criminal Court's 2009 arrest warrant for Sudanese president Omar Hassan al-Bashir?
3. According to the AI report, how many countries imprison prisoners of conscience?

A global justice gap is being made worse by power politics despite a landmark year for international justice, said Amnesty International today [May 27, 2010] in its annual assessment of human rights worldwide.

Launching *Amnesty International Report 2010: The State of the World's Human Rights*, which documents abuses in 159 countries, the organization said that powerful governments are blocking advances in international justice by standing above the law on human rights, shielding allies from criticism and acting only when politically convenient.

Governments Must Place Justice First

"Repression and injustice are flourishing in the global justice gap, condemning millions of people to abuse, oppression and poverty," said Claudio Cordone, interim secretary general of Amnesty international.

"Governments must ensure that no one is above the law, and that everyone has access to justice for all human rights violations. Until governments stop subordinating justice to political self-interest, freedom from fear and freedom from want will remain elusive for most of humanity."

Amnesty International called on governments to ensure accountability for their own actions, fully sign up to the International Criminal Court (ICC) and ensure that crimes under international law can be prosecuted anywhere in the world. It said that states claiming global leadership, including the G-20 [Group of Twenty, consisting of finance ministers and central bank governors from twenty industrialized nations], have a particular responsibility to set an example.

Amnesty International called on governments to ensure accountability for their own actions, fully sign up to the International Criminal Court (ICC) and ensure that crimes under international law can be prosecuted.

The al-Bashir Controversy

The International Criminal Court's 2009 arrest warrant for Sudanese President Omar Hassan al-Bashir, for crimes against humanity and war crimes, was a landmark event demonstrating that even sitting heads of state are not above the law. However, the African Union's refusal to cooperate, despite the nightmare of violence that has affected hundreds of thousands of people in Darfur, was a stark example of governmental failure to put justice before politics.

The UN [United Nations] Human Rights Council's paralysis over Sri Lanka, despite serious abuses including possible war crimes carried out by both government forces and the Liberation Tigers of Tamil Eelam, also stood as a testament to the international community's failure to act when needed. Meanwhile, the recommendations of the Human Rights Council's Goldstone report calling for accountability for the conflict in Gaza still need to be heeded by Israel and Hamas.

Worldwide, the justice gap sustained a pernicious web of repression. Amnesty International's research records torture or other ill-treatment in at least 111 countries, unfair trials in at least 55 countries, restrictions on free speech in at least 96 countries and prisoners of conscience imprisoned in at least 48 countries.

Human rights organizations and human rights defenders came under attack in many countries, with governments preventing their work or failing to protect them.

Areas of Concern

In the Middle East and North Africa, there were patterns of governmental intolerance of criticism in Saudi Arabia, Syria and Tunisia, and mounting repression in Iran. In Asia, the Chinese government increased pressure on challenges to its authority, detaining and harassing human rights defenders, while thousands fled severe repression and economic hardship in North Korea and [the Republic of the Union of] Myanmar [also known as Burma].

Space for independent voices and civil society shrank in parts of Europe and Central Asia, and there were unfair restrictions on freedom of expression in Russia, Turkey, Turkmenistan, Azerbaijan, Belarus and Uzbekistan. The Americas were plagued by hundreds of unlawful killings by security forces, including in Brazil, Jamaica, Colombia and Mexico, while impunity for US violations related to counterterrorism persisted. Governments in Africa such as Guinea and Madagascar met dissent with excessive use of force and unlawful killings, while Ethiopia and Uganda among others repressed criticism.

Callous disregard for civilians marked conflicts. Armed groups and government forces breached international law in the Democratic Republic of the Congo, Sri Lanka and Yemen. In the conflict in Gaza and southern Israel, Israeli forces and Palestinian armed groups unlawfully killed and injured civilians. Thousands of civilians suffered abuses in escalating violence by the Taliban in Afghanistan and Pakistan, or bore the brunt of the conflicts in Iraq and Somalia. Women and girls suffered rape and other violence carried out by government forces and armed groups in most conflicts.

Globally, with millions of people pushed into poverty by the food, energy and financial crises, events showed the urgent need to tackle the abuses that affect poverty.

Other trends included:

- Mass forced evictions of people from their homes in Africa, for example in Angola, Ghana, Kenya and Nigeria, often driving people deeper into poverty.

- Increased reports of domestic violence against women, rape, sexual abuse, and murder and mutilation after rape, in Mexico, Guatemala, El Salvador, Honduras, and Jamaica.

- Millions of migrants in Asia-Pacific countries including South Korea, Japan and Malaysia faced exploitation, violence and abuse.

- A sharp rise in racism, xenophobia and intolerance in Europe and Central Asia.

- In the Middle East and North Africa, attacks by armed groups—some apparently aligned to al Qaeda—in states such as Iraq and Yemen, heightened insecurity.

Globally, with millions of people pushed into poverty by the food, energy and financial crises, events showed the urgent need to tackle the abuses that affect poverty.

Who Should Be Held Accountable?

"Governments should be held accountable for the human rights abuses that drive and deepen poverty. The UN review meeting on the Millennium Development Goals in New York, USA, this September [2010] is an opportunity for world leaders to move from promises to legally enforceable commitments," said Claudio Cordone.

Women, especially the poor, bore the brunt of the failure to deliver on these goals. Pregnancy-related complications claimed the lives of an estimated 500,000 women, according to the most recent UN figures, with maternal mortality often directly caused by gender discrimination, violations of sexual and reproductive rights and denial of access to health care.

"Governments must promote women's equality and address discrimination against women if they are going to make progress on the Millennium Development Goals," said Claudio Cordone.

Amnesty International also called on G-20 states that have failed to fully sign up to the International Criminal Court—USA, China, Russia, Turkey, India, Indonesia, Arabia—to do so. The international review meeting on the court, beginning in Kampala, Uganda, on 31 May, is a chance for governments to show their commitment to the court.

Some Progress Has Occurred

Despite serious failures in ensuring justice last year, many events revealed progress. In Latin America, investigations into crimes shielded by amnesty laws were reopened, with landmark judgments involving former leaders including the convictions of former President Alberto Fujimori of Peru for crimes against humanity and Argentina's last military president, Reynaldo Bignone, for kidnapping and torture. All trials in the Special Court for Sierra Leone were concluded apart from the ongoing trial of former president of Liberia Charles Taylor.

"The need for effective global justice is a key lesson from the past year. Justice provides fairness and truth to those who suffer violations, deters human rights abuses and ultimately delivers a more stable and secure world," said Claudio Cordone.

2

The European Union Is Falling Short on Human Rights Commitments

Stephanie Siek

Stephanie Siek is a reporter for Deutsche Welle, *an online German news source. In the following viewpoint, she states that the 2010 Amnesty International report on human rights reveals that the countries of the European Union have not fulfilled the commitments they have made to human rights and need to improve their records on discrimination against migrants and minorities as well as torture, extraordinary rendition, and police brutality.*

As you read, consider the following questions:

1. What is the practice of "extraordinary rendition," in Siek's view?

2. According to the Amnesty International report, how has the recent economic crisis affected the issue of human rights?

3. According to Amnesty International's European Union office chief, Nicolas Beger, how many member states of the European Union have problems with racist violence and significant discrimination?

Stephanie Siek, "Amnesty International Report Says 'Justice Gap' Endangers Millions," *Deutsche Welle*, May 26, 2010. Reprinted by permission.

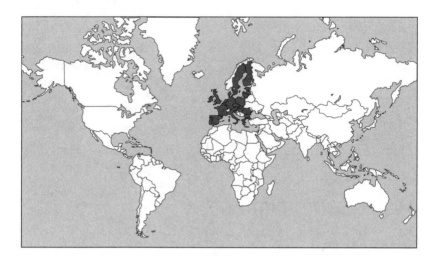

Human rights group Amnesty International said in its 2010 annual report released Thursday that a "global justice gap" allows the rights of millions to be violated while their persecutors enjoy impunity or protection.

"Governments must ensure that no one is above the law, and that everyone has access to justice for all human rights violations," Amnesty's interim Secretary General, Claudio Cordone, said in a press release. "Until governments stop subordinating justice to political self-interest, freedom from fear and freedom from want will remain elusive for most of humanity."

The report says that nations continue to protect the rights of some residents while actively denying those of others for political gain. It calls out some of the world's most powerful countries and the international community for failing to implement the ideals they proclaim, and for protecting themselves and their geopolitical allies from scrutiny when politically convenient.

Europe Has Work to Do

Western Europe fell short of its promise in several areas, the report indicates, particularly regarding the rights of migrants, minorities, and those accused of terrorism-related crimes.

National security and terrorism fears too often trumped human rights, with several European countries being involved in "extraordinary rendition," in which terrorism suspects are sent to a third country, usually one known for torture, for interrogation. Others were detained without access to legal counsel or in inadequate conditions.

Amnesty said several European states—Poland, Italy, Romania, Lithuania and Germany—had been involved in sending terrorism suspects to places where they were at risk of being tortured.

Western Europe fell short of its promise in several areas, ... particularly regarding the rights of migrants, minorities, and those accused of terrorism-related crimes.

The group also condemned Germany's practice of using "diplomatic assurances" to justify returning terrorism suspects to such countries. "Such assurances are unreliable and do not provide an effective safeguard against torture," the report said. In other cases cited in the report, German authorities made use of evidence allegedly obtained as a result of torture.

Germany was criticized for a parliamentary investigation into the country's involvement in such renditions that absolved the state of guilt, despite evidence to the contrary, Amnesty said.

Discrimination Still a Widespread Problem

Amnesty said the economic crisis had exacerbated the social exclusion of and discrimination against migrants and ethnic minorities.

"Real or perceived risks for security also continued to drive the debate," the report said, "providing fertile ground for populist rhetoric particularly in relation to migration, and exclusion of the 'other.'"

It mentions the Swiss vote to ban minarets in November 2009, as "an example of the dangers of popular initiatives transforming rights into privileges."

It specifically mentions as examples the Italian government's decision to send boats of migrants and asylum seekers to Libya, "a country with no functioning asylum procedure," after finding their boats in Mediterranean waters.

Turkey and Ukraine were criticized for forcing refugees and asylum seekers to return to countries where they might not be safe from human rights violations. Greece and Malta were called out for detaining such migrants in unacceptable conditions.

The report identifies systemic discrimination against Roma communities in several European countries: substandard schools for Roma children in Slovakia and the Czech Republic, forced evictions in Italy, Serbia and Macedonia, and assaults and murders of Roma in Hungary.

Germany was also chastised for its treatment of undocumented migrants and their children, who it said had only limited access to health care, education and legal recourse in cases where their rights as workers had been violated.

Mixed Results

The report praised the EU for the civil rights protections engendered by the EU Charter of Fundamental Rights (which the UK, Poland and the Czech Republic have opted out of in full or in part).

But it also mentioned that some member states were blocking a directive that would close a gap in antidiscrimination law for people who are discriminated against in areas other than employment, because of disability, belief, sexual orientation, religion or age.

Amnesty International's European Union office chief, Nicolas Beger, told *Deutsche Welle* that Germany was leading the charge to block the bill's passage on grounds of what he called

Human Rights Challenges in Europe

A climate of racism and intolerance in many countries fuelled ill-treatment of migrants and helped to keep them and other marginalized groups excluded from society, blocking their rights to access services, participate in government and be protected by the law. The marginalization was heightened in 2009 by fears of the economic downturn, and accompanied in many countries by a sharp rise in racism and hate speech in public discourse. The endorsement by Swiss voters in November [2009] of a constitutional ban on the construction of minarets was an example of the dangers of popular initiatives transforming rights into privileges.

Amnesty International,
"Europe and Central Asia,"
Amnesty International Report 2010:
The State of the World's Human Rights,
May 27, 2010.

"navel-gazing and petty arguments" that deny citizens in other EU countries the same protections that Germany gives its own citizens under national laws.

Germany has objected to the directive because it says previous EU antidiscrimination legislation was ineffective, and that the EU didn't have jurisdiction in all of the areas it sought to cover with the directive.

Beger said that European Union members cannot afford to be complacent about human rights just because their situation is not as severe as that in countries like Sudan or Afghanistan.

"There are 19 EU member states who still have problems with torture, ill-treatment and police brutality," Beger said. "There are 18 member states with racist violence and significant discrimination. That's not a record to be proud of."

Bangladesh Is Failing to Address Human Rights Abuses

Md. Masum Billah

Md. Masum Billah is senior manager, BRAC Education Pro-gramme, PACE. In the following viewpoint, the author reports on an instance of human rights abuse perpetrated by the Bang-ladeshi government Rapid Action Battalion (RAB) force against a reporter who spoke out against the extrajudicial killings com-mitted by this force while using the "crossfire" defense (that is, the individual began firing a weapon at the RAB, which had to respond in kind in self-defense). The author then questions the validity of the democracy when the government can control the judicial system and the police so that criminals can operate with impunity, while the jails are filled with their political victims.

As you read, consider the following questions:

1. How many extrajudicial killings have been carried out since the RAB force was formed, according to the au-thor?

2. According to the author, what is tantamount to moral bankruptcy?

3. What role does the media play in Bangladesh, according to the author?

Md. Masum Billah, "A Totalitarian Incident," *Dhaka Courier*, October 2009. www.dhakacourier.net/issue16/other/doc4.htm. Reprinted by permission.

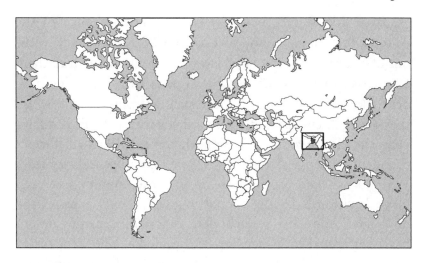

Reporter F.M. Masum of *New Age* has become the victim of torture by the elite force RAB [Rapid Action Battalion], a concoction of the previous government appreciated by the present government, though they raised their voice against the extrajudicial killings committed by this force when they were the opposition. He was picked up from his rented house in Jatrabari by some RAB officials on October 22, and brought to the RAB 10 headquarters, where he was blindfolded, and his hands were tied before a merciless beating. In addition, he was also threatened by the officers that he would be killed in 'crossfire'. Some have entitled this force as a 'notorious anti-crime force'. It is learnt that the United States and United Kingdom have over the past year provided training to RAB, in order to sensitize them to human rights. Since the establishment of this force, 1161 extrajudicial killings have taken place in their hands. Under the present government, 116 citizens have lost their lives in the name of 'crossfire' or 'counterattack'. This farce has disturbed the attention of sensible people. Extrajudicial killings bear testimony to the failure of a judicial system of the country. It proves a government's serious weakness.

How does a member of a law-enforcing agency of the country torture an honourable citizen of a democracy, without any charges against him? How can doubt alone lead them to unleash that kind of torture? How is such a horrific incident allowed to take place under state patronization? Why do they get such encouragement in a democracy? If this can happen, why did we topple [Hussain Muhammad] Ershad [former president of Bangladesh]? Why do we denounce military rule? Why do we shed crocodile tears that the country has been taken backwards by the caretaker government? What is the difference? And what is actual democracy? Inhuman treatment has been meted to a member of the media, who happens to have a voice? What tragedy can then befall the millions who don't? What were the real conditions under which 1161 people (at the time of writing) have lost their lives?

RAB simply shrugged off its responsibility with a routine expression of regret. And the RAB controlling authorities with their same 'old and traditional' expression tried to console the media men, saying 'action' will be taken against those who are responsible for this. What action, when and how they will take the action is not mentioned. That really means it will go as it has gone before. Inaction. Whenever a uniformed goon commits a crime, the government is always seen to take their side, disregarding the spirit of democracy. The country has to hide its shame from the cruel and most heinous case of Yasmin [Akhter] from Dinajpur, raped and killed by a pack of police-wolves, for surely they were beneath men. The opposition always gives false hope to the people that they turn night into day. As soon as they occupy the power, they forget the people, they forget their duties, and they forget their false promises as well. How farcical it all is!

When a government cannot take a stand against 'uniformed' criminals, it is tantamount to moral bankruptcy. If morality and intent are honest and strong, the common mass and the countrymen will stand with them. Actually what we see is that they think these armed men will save them, these armed men will stand beside them, against the people who are their enemies. Whatever they say, their actions prove otherwise. If the spirit of democracy prevails, definitely the government will talk for the people and any misdeed or crime committed by members of the law-enforcing agencies, and try them for their crimes. Otherwise, the whole of society becomes corrupt. What we witness today.

F.M. Masum begged the officer to let him bring his inhaler from the room, as he might have needed it anytime. The officer replied, "Son of a bitch. I will give you such an injection that you will never need the inhaler in your life." This is the behaviour of a member of a law-enforcing agency with a newsman, mind you. In an independent democracy. What is the point of either, it makes you wonder. A master's degree holder in journalism from Dhaka University, Masum tried to draw sympathy from the junior RAB officer, as he also claimed to be an alumnus of the same university. But in reply, he was mockingly reminded of the immunity his counterpart faced, from any punishment for killing Masum even. Where do we live? Pakistan or British India?

> Whenever a uniformed goon commits a crime, the government is always seen to take their side, disregarding the spirit of democracy.

In this country, it is the media which plays the constructive critic's role reserved for the opposition in a democracy. As we and probably many other third world countries still live in very immature democracies, this role is played by media, who try to expose the follies and vices of the society with a view to bringing positive change. It is the media which exhibits the injustice, the negligence of the state towards the poor and hapless, which extracts the ugly secrets of the powerful. Journalists take the trouble and risk their security to collect facts

Bangladesh, Torture, and Extrajudicial Killings

Impunity in Bangladesh was present at the country's birth. The 1971 war of independence was marked by atrocities on a massive scale committed against civilians, which are yet to be seriously addressed. Those who were initially detained and convicted for some of these abuses were shortly afterwards released. The scale and nature of the security forces' involvement in human rights abuses has since then varied over time, but the unwillingness of governments to hold these forces to account has been constant.

As a result, torture, killings in government custody, and other human rights violations by the police, armed forces, and the government's various paramilitary groups have become deep-rooted problems. In recent years the Rapid Action Battalion (RAB) and the military intelligence outfit, the Directorate General of Forces Intelligence (DGFI), have emerged as symbols of abuse and impunity. RAB, an elite paramilitary force created in 2004 to address public outrage over violent crime, has allegedly been responsible for over 550 killings since it began operations. Human Rights Watch and others have long alleged that many of these deaths, often described as "crossfire killings," were actually extrajudicial executions of people taken into custody. The police soon adopted these same methods, and several hundred killings have been attributed to the force over the past few years.

Human Rights Watch,
"Ignoring Executions and Torture:
Impunity for Bangladesh's Security Forces,"
May 2009.

and figures which can make them many enemies. But facing the wrath of the state, through uniformed goons, can have no place in a democracy.

Malgovernance, and the social disorder and unlimited corruption cultivated by the police has given rise to the criminals who are now being killed in 'crossfire'. Each of these deaths undermines the judiciary, a perennial victim under all our governments. The whole 'justice system' is fully controlled by the party in power. As a result, criminals go scot-free and the culture of impunity is perpetuated. Now that it has gone far beyond the controlling capacity, they start 'crossfire' or such extrajudicial steps in the name of 'quick justice'. But this kind of justice ignores the root causes. We must go deeper into the matter. Criminals should be kept in prison. Until and unless 'justice' is delivered, they must be kept in prison. But what happens here? The jails are filled with people who are the victims of political vengeance, and other minor criminals. Criminal masterminds remain free with the blessings of their powerful friends. Extrajudicial killings can never help to create a just and peaceful society.

Except for the few conscientious ones, law enforcement officials don't hesitate to commit a crime in our country. People expect that a democratic government will utilize all state forces only for the welfare of the state, not to hold citizens hostage to fear. The party in power never fails to take advantage of the opportunity. But this culture must change. Its evil traditions must be eradicated. Our votes are our weapons to this end. But as ever, our hopes are dashed.

Tibetans Are Suffering from Human Rights Abuses by China

Isaac Beech

Isaac Beech is a contributor to the Spectator. *In the following viewpoint, Beech reports on the imprisonment of Tibetan protesters by China, which uses surveillance by phone, e-mail, and other media to gain intelligence on dissidents. Tibetans are forbidden to congregate in large numbers, and Tibetan monasteries are subject to infiltration by Chinese police. Foreign journalists who attempt to report on the situation in Tibet are not given access to Tibetans to hear their story. The Chinese media portray the situation in Tibet as returning to normal and criticize the Dalai Lama for dishonesty and the West for hypocrisy.*

As you read, consider the following questions:

1. What four Chinese provinces hold approximately half of the Tibetan population?
2. According to the viewpoint, what is the Communist Party's pet phrase to describe the Dalai Lama?
3. Who is Melinda Liu and what does she say about Chinese managed press tours of Lhasa and about Chinese responses to Western media coverage of events in China and Tibet?

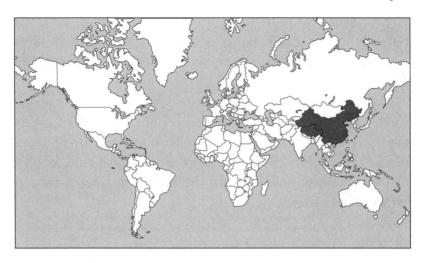

On March 14th, a Tibetan friend e-mailed me with this inscrutable message: "Here I meet many problem. Maybe you hear that. I can't say for you in the mail." March 14th seems to have been the most furious day of protests in Lhasa. That I had heard, but couldn't be sure it was the 'that' my friend was talking about.

A long silence, then I heard from him again: "Everywhere kill many Tibet here . . . Kill me no problem. I am not afraid anymore." When I finally spoke to him on the phone, I asked him if it was safe to talk about what was happening: "at this time I think that is dangerous" he muttered. Another 'that'.

I suspect it won't be until I see him in person that his evasive pronoun will ever become anything more. Nor can he be more than a pronoun himself in this article—not until the Chinese regime stops imprisoning outspoken Tibetans. Before that time (which will come, perhaps, in the Year of the Flying Pig) phones will be tapped, e-mails will be intercepted, and articles on the web will be filtered for mention of Tibet, or indeed T!bet.

The metamorphosis of my friend's voice from a guarded assurance he's OK to the attributed story of his experiences will have to wait. Tibet is in a news cocoon, impenetrable in many respects to journalists. It's a cocoon with an unhappy butterfly inside: the stories of Tibetan grievances which illustrate in human detail why protests erupted now as in 1989 and '59.

My friend lives in an ethnically Tibetan part of Qinghai, where I lived last summer. Qinghai is one of the four Chinese provinces (the others are Sichuan, Gansu and Yunnan) outside of the Tibet Autonomous Region which together hold roughly half of Tibet's population, and the historical Tibetan regions of Amdo and Kham.

A long silence, then I heard from him again: "Everywhere kill many Tibet here . . . Kill me no problem. I am not afraid anymore."

I've since learnt that his home area, which has been a hot spot of rioting, is under close surveillance. Its Tibetan population is forbidden to form large groups—quite the dampener on religious ceremonies. He himself is no stranger to oppression. In Sichuan he was arrested for a 'crime' which highlighted Tibet's historical independence from China: to specify might risk his being identified. In prison, he told me, he was fed tsampa (roasted barley flour, a Tibetan staple) with mouse droppings inside, and nearly died.

We travelled together to Labrang Monastery in Gansu, where I spoke with a monk friend of his. "Without Tibet nationality, there is no religious freedom", this monk told me, describing the incognito police who live in his monastery as Chinese monks. These, surely, are 'jackals in monks' robes', to use the Communist Party's pet phrase to describe the Dalai Lama, under whose illegal portrait we sat. When UN inspectors visited the monastery once, he claimed, Chinese officials actually did the rounds of monks' rooms putting up portraits of the Dalai Lama—only to take them down as soon as they had left.

"Bootists," cartoon by Glenn Foden, CartoonStock.com. Copyright © Glenn Foden. Reproduction rights obtainable from www.CartoonStock.com.

Up the mountainside from Labrang are the Sangke grasslands. Here we met a nomad who—judging by his unfurnished home and hard floor—was clearly not benefiting from the stream of tourists who pass through. That money goes to the Chinese: a familiar story for many Tibetans. And now my friend faces hospital bills running over 35000 RMB [Renminbi, official currency of China] (£2500) for a relative of his with organ failure from nomadic living conditions. A tall order considering his monthly salary of 1200 RMB (£90). These stories are all part of the narrative of Tibet which runs deeper than the headlines of both Chinese and Western newspapers.

"The Chinese government", one Tibetan living in London said to me recently, "thought they could pacify Tibetans with economic development or military force. Neither worked . . . China has to admit it's not winning the hearts and minds of Tibetan people." But the mouths of many Tibetans who could go into the details are closed for fear of reprisals, and the journalists who would ask the questions often can't because they are not allowed close enough.

A pack of international journalists did get close enough on March 27th—but only when thirty odd Tibetan monks broke into the room of Lhasa's Jokhang temple where they were being addressed by their Chinese government guides, and only for fifteen minutes. Then the journalists were dragged back to their babysat tour. Physically dragged, Geoff Dyer of the *Financial Times* reports.

My own visit to Lhasa was escorted too—by a Chinese tour guide, exotically named Lulu. My notes from the time describe a "despotically selective vision of Tibet". For twenty-six journalists to be shown the 'aftermath' of riots in Lhasa by a government Lulu is a tokenistic concession to free movement of the press.

Melinda Liu, President of the Foreign Correspondents' Club of China [FCCC], notes "FCCC board members do not think the brief and highly managed press tour of Lhasa satisfies Beijing Olympics' promise to allow free media reporting by foreign correspondents."

This promise—a regulation announced 1st January 2007 allowing greater freedom of movement for the foreign press in China until the Olympics—had been broken before. 180 times, according to the 2008 annual report of media rights watchdog Reporters Sans Frontières, from surveillance of journalists to arrests.

I asked a senior reporter on an official Chinese newspaper what he thought: "I don't agree with those who don't hope that journalists like you or me will cover the news in Tibet. If we let all journalists—both Chinese and foreign—cover what is happening, I think it's a good way to reduce misunderstandings."

His call was echoed the next day with the release of a petition signed by twenty-nine Chinese intellectuals, urging the

Communist Party "to allow credible national and international media to go into Tibet ... Only by adopting an open attitude can we turn around the international community's distrust of our government."

"Distrust" and "misunderstandings" are mild words compared to how the Chinese-run site www.anti-cnn.com puts it ("the lies and distorted facts of the western media"). Well, they do point out a BBC website picture of a Chinese ambulance captioned "heavy military presence in Lhasa". But on the website of *China Daily*, China's English language newspaper, you can read Wu Jiao describing "wild ducks swimming around leisurely" in a Lhasa returned to "normalcy". Which do you find more embarrassing?

At the same time, Western calls for Tibetan independence (rather than autonomy) play right into the Chinese government's hands: they can be dismissed as 'splittist' to this generation of nationalistic young Chinese.

If wild ducks have a higher billing than angry monks, these protests run the risk of being brushed under the carpet—like the cursory sentence on the 1959 riots in the book *China's Tibet* I read in Beijing. I chatted online to a Chinese friend in Beijing, who typed "it seems a bit strange. I think people on one side don't know about [the riots] and on the other side don't think it's going to be a huge problem. The only news I can obtain is from *China Daily*, which you know. . ."

For *China Daily* to run headlines like "Media must be objective" next to "Dalai Lama not an honest man" hardly puts them in a credible position to follow up with "Bold hypocrisy of the Western world". Melinda Liu comments "the recent allegations of Western media conspiracies to tarnish China are a reflection of growing nationalism among Chinese . . . unaccustomed to hearing international criticism of the Chinese government. That's partly because of the filtered nature of information flow, due to censored traditional media, imprisonment of cyber-dissidents, and sophisticated Internet policing technologies."

At the same time, Western calls for Tibetan independence (rather than autonomy) play right into the Chinese government's hands: they can be dismissed as 'splittist' to this generation of nationalistic young Chinese. Nor should Tibetan violence against Han Chinese and Hui Muslim be glossed over by the international media in favour of the more sellable red face of Chinese oppression (www.ourvoice.de is a less shouty attack on Western coverage).

A Tibet open to Chinese journalists will increase international respect for China's Communist Party and educate a lot of Chinese about truths withheld from them. A Tibet open to foreign journalists will bring stories from the attic of the world out from under the rafters and lend nuance to the reporting of crisis in Shangri-La.

And if Tibet remains tightly closed? As the Beijing correspondent of a US newspaper told me, "when you bar reporters from an area, we are constitutionally created to find out why ... It would be a sad abdication of our responsibilities if we didn't. If China begins the Olympics from a defensive crouch," he said, "I will not write of it as a brilliant debut."

The Arab World Is Experiencing a Deterioration of Human Rights

Cairo Institute for Human Rights Studies

The Cairo Institute for Human Rights Studies is an independent nongovernmental organization that studies and disseminates information about the state of human rights in the Arab world. In the following viewpoint, the institute reports that the human rights situation in the Arab world deteriorated in 2009, with many abuses against women, ethnic and religious minorities, and refugees. The institute also notes a lack of accountability for such crimes in the region.

As you read, consider the following questions:

1. How many Arab countries does the report by the Cairo Institute for Human Rights Studies cover?
2. How many Palestinians were killed during the blockade and invasion of Gaza in 2009?
3. How many years has Syria been under emergency law as of 2009?

"Embrace diversity, end discrimination"

—*Human Rights Day 2009*

Cairo Institute for Human Rights Studies, "Reports & Analyses on Bastion of Impunity, Mirage of Reform: Human Rights in the Arab World: Annual Report 2009," Cairo Institute for Human Rights Studies, August 12, 2009. Reprinted by permission.

"A man spends his first years learning how to speak and the Arab regimes teach him silence for the rest of his life"

—*Algerian writer Ahlem Mosteghanemi,*
Memory in the Flesh

Today [August 12, 2009], the Cairo Institute for Human Rights Studies released its second annual report on the state of human rights in the Arab world for the year 2009. The report ... concludes that the human rights situation in the Arab region has deteriorated throughout the region over the last year.

The report reviews the most significant developments in human rights during 2009 in 12 Arab countries: Egypt, Tunisia, Algeria, Morocco, Sudan, Lebanon, Syria, Palestine, Iraq, Saudi Arabia, Bahrain, and Yemen. It also devotes separate chapters to the Arab League and an analysis of the performance of Arab governments in UN [United Nations] human rights institutions. Another chapter addresses the stance of Arab governments concerning women's rights, the limited progress made to advance gender equality, and how Arab governments use the issue of women's rights to burnish their image before the international community while simultaneously evading democratic and human rights reform measures required to ensure dignity and equality for all of their citizens.

The Situation in Palestine

The report observes the grave and ongoing Israeli violations of Palestinian rights, particularly the collective punishment of Palestinians in the Gaza Strip through the ongoing blockade and the brutal invasion of Gaza at the beginning of 2009 which resulted in the killing of more than 1,400 Palestinians, 83 percent of them civilians not taking part in hostilities. The report notes that the plight of the Palestinian people has been exacerbated by the Fatah-Hamas conflict [a civil war between two main Palestinian parties], which has turned universal rights and liberties into favors granted on the basis of political affiliation. Both parties have committed grave abuses against their opponents, including arbitrary detention, lethal torture, and extrajudicial killings.

The deterioration in Yemeni affairs may presage the collapse of what remains of the central state structure due to policies that give priority to the monopolization of power and wealth, corruption that runs rampant, and a regime that continues to deal with opponents using solely military and security means. As such, Yemen is now the site of a war in the northern region of Saada, a bloody crackdown in the south, and social and political unrest throughout the country. Moreover, independent press and human rights defenders who expose abuses in both the north and south are targets of increasingly harsh repression.

The Situation in the Sudan

In its blatant contempt for justice, the Sudanese regime is the exemplar for impunity and the lack of accountability. President [Omar al-]Bashir has refused to appear before the International Criminal Court in connection with war crimes in Darfur. Instead, his regime is hunting down anyone in the country who openly rejects impunity for war crimes, imprisoning and torturing them and shutting down rights organizations. Meanwhile the government's policy of collective punishment against the population of Darfur continues, as well as its evasion of responsibilities under the Comprehensive Peace Agreement between the north and south, making secession a more likely scenario, which may once again drag the country into a bloody civil war.

In Lebanon, the threat of civil war that loomed last year [2008] has receded, but the country still suffers from an entrenched two-tier power structure in which Hezbollah's superior military capabilities give the opposition an effective veto. As a result, the state's constitutional institutions have been paralyzed.

In this context it took several months for the clear winner in the parliamentary elections to form a government. Now, even after the formation of a government, the unequal military balance of power between the government and the opposition will prevent serious measures to guarantee all parties accountable before the law, and greatly undermine the possibility of delivering justice for the many crimes and abuses experienced by the Lebanese people over the last several years.

The [Sudanese] government's policy of collective punishment against the population of Darfur continues, as well as its evasion of responsibilities under the Comprehensive Peace Agreement between the north and south.

Iraq Has Seen Improvement

Although Iraq is still the largest arena of violence and civilian deaths, it witnessed a relative improvement in some areas, though these gains remain fragile. The death toll has dropped and threats against journalists are less frequent. In addition, some of the major warring factions have indicated they are prepared to renounce violence and engage in the political process.

In Egypt, as the state of emergency approaches the end of its third decade, the broad immunity given to the security apparatus has resulted in the killing of dozens of undocumented migrants, the use of lethal force in the pursuit of criminal suspects, and routine torture. Other signs of deterioration were visible in 2009: The emergency law was applied broadly to repress freedom of expression, including detaining or abducting bloggers. Moreover, the Egyptian police state is increasingly acquiring certain theocratic features, which have reduced some religious freedoms, and have led to an unprecedented expansion of sectarian violence within the country.

In Tunisia, the authoritarian police state continued its unrestrained attacks on political activists, journalists, human rights defenders, trade unionists, and others involved in social protest. At the same time, the political stage was prepared for the reelection of President [Zine El Abidine] Ben Ali through the introduction of constitutional amendments that disqualified any serious contenders.

In Algeria, the emergency law, the Charter for Peace and National Reconciliation, and the application of counterterrorism measures entrenched policies of impunity, grave police abuses, and the undermining of accountability and freedom of expression. Constitutional amendments paved the way for the installment of President [Abdelaziz] Bouteflika as president for life amid elections that were contested on many levels, despite the lack of real political competition.

The Worsening Situation in Morocco

Morocco, unfortunately, has seen a tangible erosion of the human rights gains achieved by Moroccans over the last decade. A fact most clearly seen in the failure of the government to adopt a set of institutional reforms within the security and judicial sectors intended to prevent impunity for crimes. Morocco's relatively improved status was also undermined by the intolerance shown for freedom of expression, particularly for expression touching on the king or the royal family, or instances of institutional corruption. Protests against the status of the Moroccan-administered Western Sahara region were also repressed and several Sahrawi activists were referred to a military tribunal for the first time in 14 years.

As Syria entered its 47th year of emergency law, it continued to be distinguished by its readiness to destroy all manner of political opposition, even the most limited manifestations

"The Swiss voters backed minarets ban . . . ," cartoon by Karsten Schley, CartoonStock .com. Copyright © Karsten Schley. Reproduction rights available from www.Cartoon Stock.com.

of independent expression. The Kurdish minority was kept in check by institutionalized discrimination, and human rights defenders were targets for successive attacks. Muhannad al-Hassani, the president of the Sawasiya human rights organization, was arrested and tried, and his attorney, Haitham al-Maleh, the former chair of the Syrian Human Rights Association, was referred to a military tribunal. The offices of the Syrian Center for Media and Freedom of Expression were shut down, and Syrian prisons still hold dozens of prisoners of conscience and democracy advocates.

Bahrain Suffers from Widespread Human Rights Abuses

In Bahrain, the systematic discrimination against the Shiite majority was accompanied by more repression of freedom of expression and peaceful assembly. Human rights defenders increasingly became targets for arrest, trial, and smear campaigns. Some human rights defenders were even subjected by government agents to threats and intimidation while in Europe.

In Saudi Arabia, the report notes that the monarch's speeches urging religious tolerance and interfaith dialogue abroad have not been applied inside the kingdom, where the religious police continue to clamp down on personal freedom. Indeed, repression of religious freedoms is endemic, and the Shiite minority continues to face systematic discrimination. Counterterrorism policies were used to justify long-term arbitrary detention, and political activists advocating reform were tortured. These policies also undermined judicial standards, as witnessed by the prosecution of hundreds of people in semi-secret trials over the last year.

Various Arab governments and members of the Organization of the Islamic Conference have been working in concert within UN institutions to undermine international mechanisms and standards for the protection of human rights.

Arab Governments Undermine Justice

In tandem with these grave abuses and the widespread lack of accountability for such crimes within Arab countries, the report notes that various Arab governments and members of the Organization of the Islamic Conference have been working in concert within UN [United Nations] institutions to undermine international mechanisms and standards for the protection of human rights. On this level, Arab governments have sought to undercut provisions that bring governments to account or seriously assess and monitor human rights. This is most clearly illustrated by the broad attack on independent UN human rights experts and NGOs [nongovernmental organizations] working within the UN, as well as attempts to legalize international restrictions on freedom of expression through the pretext of prohibiting "defamation of religions."

In the same vein, the Arab League and its summit forums offered ongoing support for the Bashir regime in Sudan despite charges of war crimes, and members of the organization used the principle of national sovereignty as a pretext to remain silent about or even collaborate on grave violations in several Arab states. Little hope should be invested in the Arab League as a protector of human rights regionally. Indeed, the Arab Commission for Human Rights, created by the Arab Charter on Human Rights (a weak document compared to other regional charters), is partially composed of government officials, and the secretariat of the Arab League has begun to take measures to weaken the commission, including obstructing the inclusion of NGOs in its work, intentionally undermining its ability to engage in independent action, even within the stifling constraints laid out by the charter.

Israel Is Violating International Law and the Human Rights of Palestinians

John Dugard

John Dugard is a South African professor of international law and has served as judge ad hoc on the International Court of Justice. In the following viewpoint, he argues that Israel is guilty of human rights violations. Dugard identifies Israel's worst crimes as those perpetrated against the Palestinian people: systematic discrimination, torture, forced relocation, and ethnic cleansings. This text is Dugard's keynote address for the "Israel and the International Law" conference of November 2009 in Beirut, Lebanon.

As you read, consider the following questions:

1. What institutions have held Israel to be in violation of international law?

2. According to Dugard, is there substantial evidence to prove that Israel tortures Palestinians?

3. How does Dugard compare Israel's discriminatory and repressive practices to apartheid in South Africa?

The dispute over Palestine is a political one but it is conducted within a legal framework. From the outset—the notorious [United Nations] Partition Plan [for Palestine in

John Dugard, "International Law, Israel and Palestine," Afro-Middle East Centre, March 18, 2010. Reprinted by permission.

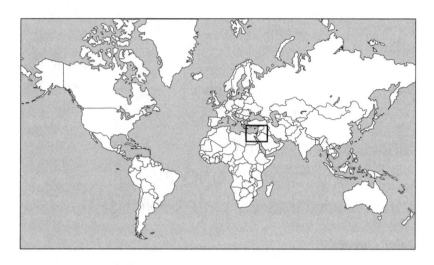

1947] contained in General Assembly Resolution 181 (II) [which created the modern state of Israel]—international law has played an important role in the dispute. Today, the dispute is probably more characterized by legal argument than at any time before. It is, therefore, appropriate to consider the dispute in legal terms, as we shall be doing in this conference ["Israel and the International Law"].

Since the declaration of the state of Israel over sixty years ago Israel has consistently been in violation of international law. Over the years it has violated—and is still violating—some of the most fundamental norms of international law. It has been held to be in violation of international law by the [United Nations] Security Council, the General Assembly, the Human Rights Council, human rights treaty monitoring bodies and the International Court of Justice. In this respect it resembles apartheid in South Africa which for over forty years violated international law by practicing racial discrimination, engaging in political repression, manufacturing nuclear weapons and carrying out military offensives against its neighbours. But there the similarity ends.

South Africa was subjected to an arms embargo by the Security Council, to all sorts of sanctions by the General Assembly and by nation-states. It was isolated by the international community in trade, sport, education and cultural life. Ultimately it succumbed to international pressure and abandoned apartheid. Israel on the other hand, remains a friend of the West and has been subjected to little pressure to conform to international standards. Why? And what are the consequences? These are some of the things I wish to speak about today.

In approaching this subject I will consider three issues. First, the principal legal norms that have been violated. Secondly, the response of the international community and why Israel is a protected state. Thirdly, what the consequences of the present situation are for world peace in general and human rights in particular.

Since the declaration of the state of Israel over sixty years ago Israel has consistently been in violation of international law.

The Principal Legal Norms Violated by Israel

Ethnic cleansing is one of the most heinous of international crimes. It is certainly a crime against humanity and it may constitute genocide. The ethnic cleansing of Palestinians from the newly formed state of Israel in 1948 was originally portrayed by Israel as the "voluntary departure" of hundreds of thousands of Palestinians to neighbouring states. Today the historical record of the Nakba has been more carefully scrutinized by [Israeli history professor and political activist] Ilan Pappe (*The Ethnic Cleansing of Palestine* [2006]) and others and there can be no doubt that Israel in a cruel and calculated manner drove some 750,000 Palestinians from their homes by a process of terror and violence. To aggravate matters Israel ignored, and still ignores, General Assembly Resolution 194(III) of 11 December 1948 which declares that refugees should be allowed to return to their homes and compensation should be paid in the case of those not wishing to return. Despite the fact that Israel in its first year of existence had committed crimes against humanity in a systematic manner and refused to comply with the General Assembly's prescription for the solution to the Palestinian refugee problem, it was admitted to the United Nations [UN] as a "peace loving state" that was "able and willing to carry out the obligations contained in the Charter" on 11 May 1949. From the very beginning therefore the international community turned a blind eye to Israel's crimes and indicated that it was to be protected and promoted however badly it behaved.

Israel's 1956 Sinai campaign [against Egypt] was hailed in Israel (and Britain and France) as a defensive and just war. But, again, recent studies with full access to the historical materials have reached a different conclusion. The Israeli historian, Avi Shlaim, argues that Israel, Britain and France engaged in a "tripartite aggression" that had disastrous political consequences. What is striking about this failed adventure is that Britain, despite its reservations about the creation of the state of Israel in 1948/49 was prepared to involve Israel as an ally in an aggressive war.

Time does not permit me to enter into the debate of whether Israel acted in self-defence or whether it was the aggressor in the 1967 Six-Day War. Suffice it to say that after the war the Security Council passed Resolution 242 in which it affirmed that the principles of the UN Charter required "the withdrawal of Israel armed forces from territories occupied in the recent conflict". Israel has refused to heed this call and has instead formally annexed East Jerusalem and the Golan Heights and refused to withdraw from the West Bank and Gaza. To date no state has recognized Israel's annexation of East Jerusalem and the Golan Heights which demonstrates the degree of international consensus on the illegality of Israel's annexations. Israel has sought to justify its failure to withdraw from the territories that it occupied in 1967 except Sinai on the specious ground that the resolution does not require Israel to withdraw from "all" territories occupied and therefore permits Israel to annex portions of the West Bank. Careful studies on this subject, that examine the historical record, again show that Israel's arguments are simply wrong.

From the very beginning ... the international community turned a blind eye to Israel's crimes and indicated that it was to be protected and promoted however badly it behaved.

Israel and the Geneva Convention

The international community is united in its belief that the Fourth Geneva Convention of 1949 is binding on Israel in respect of its treatment of the West Bank, East Jerusalem and Gaza. This belief is founded on sound legal principle and the interpretation of the convention. But, again, Israel has raised specious legal arguments to justify its refusal to apply the convention in the occupied territories, claiming that the occupation did not result in the occupation of territory of a sovereign state and this renders the Fourth Geneva Convention inapplicable. Despite the unanimity of the international community on this subject, the Israeli government refuses to budge. Not even the 2004 advisory opinion of the International Court of Justice on the Wall—unanimous on this subject—has persuaded Israel to accept the rules of international law. Which is not surprising as Israel's promotion of settlements in the West Bank (and previously Gaza) is premised on the nonbinding force of the Fourth Geneva Convention.

Israel's refusal to stop the construction of settlements is a clear violation of Article 49(6) of the Fourth Geneva Convention. The international community is agreed on this. There is no support for Israel's ridiculous interpretations of the provision; and not even the Israeli Supreme Court, usually prepared to give support to government positions, has endorsed the government's position. But this, the international community has failed to take meaningful action, despite the fact that the continued construction of settlements makes a two-state solution increasingly nonviable.

Israel is in violation of many other provisions of the Fourth Geneva Convention, ranging from the violation of collective punishment (Article 33) to the destruction of property and demolition of homes not justified by military necessity (Article 53). What is often forgotten is that the convention and customary international law require Israel to ensure the health and educational needs of the occupied people and to provide adequate food and medicines for them (Articles 50, 55 and 56). Israel completely fails to comply with these obligations and instead relies on the international donor community and tunnel smugglers to fulfill its obligations. Of course the donor community is in an awkward situation: On the one hand, it knows that it is protecting Israel but on the other hand it knows that if it does nothing the Palestinian people will suffer.

Israel and Nuclear Weapons

Sometime in the 1970s Israel, together with apartheid South Africa, started to develop and manufacture nuclear weapons. In the early 1990s South Africa destroyed its nuclear arsenal. But Israel has retained its nuclear weapons. Unlike Iran, Israel is not a party to the Nuclear Non-Proliferation Treaty (NPT). So, unlike Iran it cannot be accused of being in violation of its obligations under this treaty. The law governing possession of nuclear weapons is unclear but there can be little doubt that customary international law prohibits the undisclosed manufacture of nuclear weapons. The attitude of the West towards Israel and Iran in this respect reveals just how far the double standard has gone. Sanctions are imposed on Iran for, perhaps, taking steps to develop nuclear weapons and failing to comply with its obligations under the NPT; but nothing happens to Israel which has nuclear weapons and fails to account for its possession of such weapons (unlike India and Pakistan).

Israel's violation of human rights treaties requires special mention. Israel is a party to the two international covenants, the Convention on the Elimination of All Forms of Discrimination [Against Women], the Convention on the Rights of the Child and the torture convention. Its claims that these conventions do not govern its conduct in the occupied Palestinian territory have been rejected by both the monitoring bodies of these treaties and by the International Court of Justice. Israel's violations of these treaties have been affirmed and documented by both monitoring bodies and the International Court of Justice.

The violation of the prohibitions on discrimination, torture and the right to life are particularly important.

Israel Is Violating International Law

Discrimination is condemned by all international human rights conventions. Israel actively discriminates against Palestinians in many fields, particularly in respect of freedom of movement. Checkpoints can be compared to the hated pass system of apartheid South Africa, but the separate roads for settlers and Palestinians find no precedent in apartheid South Africa. Considerations of this kind explain why South Africans, black and white, who visit Palestine, routinely declare that the situation in Palestine is worse than it was in apartheid South Africa.

Today the prohibition on torture is seen as a cardinal principle of international law, one that enjoys the status of *jus cogens* [compelling law] and constitutes a crime against humanity. States that practice torture are widely castigated. But not Israel, despite the fact that there is substantial evidence that its security forces routinely and systematically engage in torture of Palestinian detainees. So too Israel's practice of murdering political opponents, euphemistically described as targeted killings. If any other state resorted to such practices against their political opponents there would be international outrage. But in the case of Israel it is accepted and states continue to supply Israel with sophisticated weaponry to allow it to continue with this practice.

Israel actively discriminates against Palestinians in many fields, particularly in respect of freedom of movement.

The Wall That Separates Israel and Palestinian West Bank

The Wall. I have seen many sections of the Wall. As special rapporteur on human rights in the occupied Palestinian territory I made a special point of visiting the Wall and speaking to farmers and communities affected by the Wall. I have no doubt that the primary purpose of the Wall is the de facto annexation of Palestinian land in order to include eighty per cent of the settler population within Israel and to promote the "Judaization" of Jerusalem. Israel's initial claim that it is a "security fence" was from the outset difficult to reconcile with the construction of the Wall within Palestinian territory instead of along the Green Line. But in recent times even Israel has dropped this argument and today unashamedly admits that its main purpose is to redraw the boundaries of Israel to include most settlements. The International Court of Justice has held the Wall to be illegal on the ground that it violates both the Fourth Geneva Convention and human rights conventions and called on Israel to dismantle the Wall and to pay compensation to those whose land has been seized. . . . The international community's response has been weak—timid—to put it kindly. No attempt has been made to enforce the opinion. I will say more about this shortly.

Israel is determined to change the character of Jerusalem and to transform it from the centre of Palestinian life into a

Jewish city. Houses are unlawfully demolished, the Wall is constructed through Jerusalem's neighbourhoods dividing families in the process, and access to religious sites is seriously curtailed. Even the Holy City is not exempt from Israel's illegal land grab.

Finally, in this superficial and inadequate litany of Israel's sins, there are its military incursions into Gaza and the West Bank since 2000, into Lebanon in 2006 and, above all, its assault on Gaza in 2008/2009 in Operation Cast Lead. As chair of the Arab League Independent Fact-Finding Committee on Gaza (IFFC), which visited Gaza in February 2009, I had occasion to see the destruction caused by the IDF [Israel Defense Forces] and to speak to victims. The IFFC had no hesitation in finding that Israel had committed war crimes and crimes against humanity in Operation Cast Lead. It considered the question of genocide as on the face of it, genocide appeared to have been committed.

Collective Punishment Was the Goal

But we found that the purpose of the offensive was collective punishment and that Israel lacked the special intent to destroy a people required for the crime of genocide.

Other investigations conducted by Human Rights Watch, Amnesty International, Physicians for Human Rights, B'Tselem, the Martin Commission appointed by the UN secretary-general to investigate IDF attacks on UN premises in Gaza, and, above all, the Goldstone mission appointed by the Human Rights Council, have all reached similar conclusions. Israel has not seriously challenged the substance of any of these reports. Instead it has criticized the messengers and the Human Rights Council. Most recently it has suggested changing the laws of war to allow Israel to commit crimes in the name of the so-called war against terror. This seems to be a clear indication that Israel admits that it did commit crimes in Gaza. The evidence is abundantly clear: Israel committed serious violations of international humanitarian law and human rights law in the course of Operation Cast Lead; and its political and military leaders committed war crimes and crimes against humanity in the operation.

How does one categorize Israel? In the first place, its denial of the right of self-determination of the Palestinian people, its exploitation of Palestinian resources (particularly water), its subjugation of the Palestinian people and its settlement practices and policies require that it be seen as a colonial state in a world which has outlawed colonialism. Secondly, as a study conducted by the South African Human Sciences Research Council . . . convincingly shows, Israel's discriminatory and repressive practices fall within the prohibitions contained in the 1973 [International] Convention on the Suppression and Punishment of the Crime of Apartheid and resemble, but go beyond, apartheid South Africa. Thirdly, Israel is a state with a criminal record. The International Law Commission in its Draft Articles on the Responsibility of States for Internationally Wrongful Acts of 2001 refrained from dealing with questions of international crimes with the result that the notion of state criminal responsibility is uncertain. But how does one describe a state that practises colonialism and apartheid and is guilty of serious war crimes and crimes against humanity. Surely it must be seen as a criminal state?

The Response of the International Community with Special Reference to the West

Time does not permit me to examine the practice of the entire international community to Israel's conduct. The developing world is united in its hostility to Israel, as is reflected in voting on Israel in the Human Rights Council. But this is not a high priority and most countries of Asia, Africa and Latin America are unwilling to risk the advantages of good relations with the West by espousing the Palestinian cause too vigorously. I do not sufficiently understand the politics of the Arab world to pronounce on the Arab response. Suffice it to say that while Arabs on the street are desperately concerned about Israel's actions this mood is not reflected in government actions. Clearly Arab states could do more, much more, to help Palestinians both politically and materially. One suspects that many leaders are unwilling to risk their relationship with Washington [D.C.] for the sake of the Palestinians.

To aggravate matters, the Palestinians provide no leadership. The division between Fatah and Hamas [Palestinian and Islamic resistance groups] and the failure of the Palestinian [National] Authority to give a coherent lead, as crudely illustrated by [chairman of the Palestine Liberation Organization, Mahmoud] Abbas's recent performance over the Goldstone mission report make it difficult for Arab states to know what Palestinians want. In these circumstances I shall focus on the response of the West.

The West's Weak Response

The West, and particularly Western Europe, is acutely aware of the sufferings of the Palestinian people and the injustices of the situation. European missions in Ramallah and East Jerusalem report accurately to their governments on the situation as do many European-based NGOs [nongovernmental organizations]. These governments show their concern by funding humanitarian projects in Palestine on a large scale. European public opinion is also largely sympathetic to the Palestinian cause and supports NGOs working on humanitarian programmes in the region. Without this assistance Palestine would not survive. But it is at the political level, in the United Nations, particularly the Quartet [on the Middle East], Security Council, General Assembly and Human Rights Council, that their performance must be judged.

Ultimately the political policies of the West towards Israel are determined by Washington, and the policies of Washington are determined by the Israel lobby, comprising both American Jewish organizations (notably AIPAC [American Israel Public Affairs Committee, America's pro-Israel lobby] and the Anti-Defamation League) and Christian evangelicals. The European Union [EU] and most European states follow Washington's lead blindly. Feelings of Holocaust guilt probably play a role in European decision making, but essentially Europe follows the United States.

The two-state solution, improved relations with the Moslem world and the universality of human rights are all sacrificial lambs that may be slaughtered and offered on the alter of appeasement of Israel.

The West is determined to avoid the kind of showdown that it had in the case of South Africa with Israel. In the Security Council, the United States uses its veto to protect Israel, with or without the assistance of France and Britain. In the Quartet established informally by the Security Council to promote the peace process in the Middle East, comprising the UN, the US, EU and Russian Federation, Washington takes the lead and ensures that no strong action is taken against Israel. This starkly illustrated by the attitude of the Quartet towards the Wall opinion. The UN, EU and Russian Federation all gave their approval to the Court's opinion in the General Assembly in 2004, but the Quartet has failed to even mention the Wall opinion in its regular three monthly statements let alone take action to persuade or compel Israel to comply with its findings. The reason for this is clear. The United States has consistently opposed the opinion and is determined not to give effect to it. The UN, led by a secretary-general unable to stand up to Washington, the EU and the Russian Federation are unwilling to challenge Washington, despite any commitment they may have to the rule of law and human rights. . . .

The Consequences of the West's Failure to Act Against Israel

No immediate consequences outside Palestine will follow from the West's failure to take action against Israel. The situation in Palestine itself will continue as it does today. The Quartet will continue to promote its defunct road map, which means appealing to Israel to stop building settlements and to behave well, and to Palestine to take tougher action against "terrorists", without any threat of sanction. The Security Council will continue to debate the issue without threat of sanction. This will allow Israel to increase its settler population in the West Bank, intensify its stranglehold on the Jordan Valley, complete the "Judaization" of Jerusalem, finish construction of the Wall and its annexation of some thirteen per cent of Palestinian land, and maintain its blockade of Gaza, supported by regular military incursions.

The long-term consequences are more serious. If Israel is allowed to proceed as it is at present, a two-state solution will become impossible and the West will have to confront the only viable alternative: a single state with a Palestinian majority. Then it will have to decide whether to support an apartheid state solution in which the Jewish minority has power over a Palestinian majority or to insist on majority rule in a democratic state. While this process is under way public opinion in Arab states will intensify and "moderate" Arab governments will be replaced by more radical regimes. Relations between the West and the Moslem world will further deteriorate as a result of the West's perceived support for Israel. And human rights will lose credibility as a result of the West's continued protection of Israel and its failure to hold Israel accountable for its actions. Already the double standard displayed by the West in its protection of Israel has had consequences: The developing world refuses to police its own human rights violators in the face of the West determination to shield Israel from criticism for its human rights violations. This, essentially, is what is happening in the Human Rights Council: The developing world uses the council as a vehicle to condemn Israel; and protects its own human rights offenders from scrutiny because of the West's protection of Israel.

But the West appears to be undeterred by these consequences. For it, protection of the Jewish state is paramount whatever the cost. The two-state solution, improved relations with the Moslem world and the universality of human rights are all sacrificial lambs that may be slaughtered and offered on the alter of appeasement of Israel.

The United States Must Face Its Own Record of Human Rights Abuses

China Daily

China Daily *is a Chinese daily newspaper. In the following viewpoint, the author reports on the Chinese government's publication of the* Human Rights Record of the United States in 2007, *which chronicles numerous violations of human rights in the United States and by its citizens abroad. The author argues that the United States should get its own act together before it starts criticizing China.*

As you read, consider the following questions:

1. The Chinese report on the U.S. human rights record claims the United States attacks how many countries regarding human rights issues?
2. How many U.S. citizens were living in poverty in 2006, according to the report?
3. How does the report feel that American women are being discriminated against?

China issued on Thursday [in March 2008] the *Human Rights Record of the United States in 2007* in response to the *Country Reports on Human Rights Practices* for 2007 issued by the US Department of State on Tuesday.

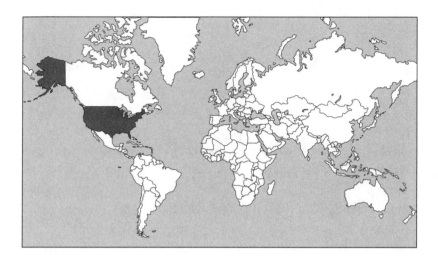

Released by the Information Office of China's State Council, the Chinese report listed a multitude of cases to show the human rights situation in the United States and its violation of human rights in other countries.

The report says the United States attacks more than 190 countries and regions including China on their human rights issues, but mentions nothing about its own human rights problems.

By publishing the *Human Rights Record of the United States in 2007*, the report says it aims to "help the people have a better understanding of the real situation in the United States and as a reminder for the United States to reflect upon its own issues".

The report reviewed the human rights record of the United States in 2007 from seven perspectives: on life and personal security; on human rights violations by law enforcement and judicial departments; on civil and political rights; on economic, social and cultural rights; on racial discrimination; on rights of women and children and on the United States' violation of human rights in other countries.

The report says the increase of violent crimes in the United States poses a serious threat to its people's lives, liberty and personal security.

Violent Crime in the United States

According to an FBI [Federal Bureau of Investigation] report on crime statistics released in September 2007, 1.41 million violent crimes were reported nationwide in 2006, an increase of 1.9 percent over 2005.

Of the violent crimes, the estimated number of murders and no negligent manslaughters increased 1.8 percent, and that of robberies increased 7.2 percent.

Throughout 2006, US residents age 12 or above experienced an estimated 25 million crimes of violence and theft, according to the FBI report.

In the United States, about 30,000 people die from gun wounds every year, according to a Reuters story on December 19, 2007.

The *USA Today* reported on December 5, 2007, gun killings have climbed 13 percent overall since 2002.

On April 16, 2007, the Virginia Tech University witnessed the deadliest shooting rampage in modern US history with 33 killed and more than 30 others injured, according to AFP [a French news agency].

Two separate gun killings in Salt Lake City and Philadelphia claimed eight lives and injured several other people on February 12, 2007, according to the Associated Press.

Abuses by Law Enforcement

The report points out that law enforcement and judicial departments in the United States have abused their power and seriously violated the freedom and rights of its citizens.

Cases in which US law enforcement authorities allegedly violated victims' civil rights increased by 25 percent from fis-

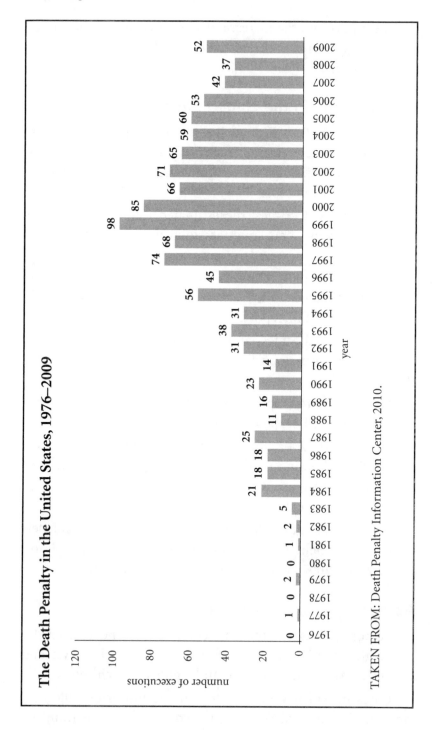

The Death Penalty in the United States, 1976–2009

TAKEN FROM: Death Penalty Information Center, 2010.

cal year 2001 to 2007 over the previous seven years, according to statistics from the US Department of Justice.

However, the majority of law enforcement officers accused of brutality were not prosecuted in the end.

Cases in which US law enforcement authorities allegedly violated victims' civil rights increased by 25 percent from fiscal year 2001 to 2007 over the previous seven years.

From May 2001 to June 2006, 2,451 police officers in Chicago received 4 to 10 complaints each, 662 of them received more than 10 complaints each, but only 22 were punished. Furthermore, there were officers who had amassed more than 50 abuse complaints but were never disciplined in any fashion, according to statistics released by the University of Chicago.

The United States of America is the world's largest prison and has the highest inmates/population ratio in the world. A December 5, 2007, report by EFE [Spanish] news agency quoted statistics of the US Department of Justice as saying that the number of inmates in US prisons have increased by 500 percent over the last 30 years.

The Right to Unionize

The freedom and rights of individual citizens are being increasingly marginalized in the United States, the report says.

Workers' right to unionize has been restricted in the United States. It was reported that union membership fell by 326,000 in 2006, bringing the percentage of employees in unions to 12 percent, down from 20 percent in 1983.

Employer resistance stopped 53 percent of nonunion workers from joining a union, the *New York Times* reported on January 26, 2007.

According to a report by the Human Rights Watch, when Wal-Mart stores faced unionization drives, the company often broke the law by, for example, eavesdropping on workers, turning surveillance cameras on them and firing those who favored unions.

Hypocrisy of the US Democratic System

In the United States, money is "mother's milk" for politics while elections are "games" for the wealthy, highlighting the hypocrisy of the US democracy, which has been fully borne out by the 2008 presidential election.

The "financial threshold" for participating in the US presidential election is becoming higher and higher. At least 10 of the 20-strong major party candidates who are seeking the US presidency in general elections in 2008 are millionaires, according to a report by Spanish news agency EFE on May 18, 2007.

The French news agency AFP reported on January 15, 2007, that the 2008 presidential election will be the most expensive race in history. The cost of the last presidential campaign in 2004, considered a peak for its time, was 693 million US dollars. Common estimates of this year's total outlay have tended to come in at around 1 billion US dollars, and *Fortune* magazine recently upped its overall cost projection to 3 billion US dollars.

Freedom of the Press?

The US administration manipulated the press. On October 23, 2007, the Federal Emergency Management Agency (FEMA) staged a news conference on California wildfires.

A half-dozen questions were asked within 15 minutes at the event by FEMA staff members posing as reporters.

The news was aired by US-based television stations. After the *Washington Post* disclosed the farce, FEMA tried to defend itself for staging the fake briefing.

The report says that the deserved economic, social and cultural rights of US citizens have not been properly protected.

Poverty in America

Poor population in the United States is constantly increasing.

According to statistics released by the US Census Bureau in August 2007, the official poverty rate in 2006 was 12.3 percent.

There were 36.5 million people, or 7.7 million families living in poverty in 2006. In another word, almost one out of eight US citizens lives in poverty.

The wealth of the richest group in the United States has rapidly expanded in recent years, widening the earning gap between the rich and poor. The earnings of the highest one percent of the population accounted for 21.2 percent of US total national income in 2005, compared with 19 percent in 2004.

The earnings of the lowest 50 percent of the population accounted for 12.8 percent of the total national income in 2005, down from 13.4 percent in 2004, according to Reuters.

Hunger and Homelessness

Hungry and homeless people have increased significantly in US cities. The US Department of Agriculture said in a report released on November 14, 2007, that at least 35.5 million people in the United States, including 12.63 million children, went hungry in 2006, an increase of 390,000 from 2005.

About 11 million people lived in "very low food security", according to Reuters.

People without health insurance have been increasing in the United States. A Reuters report on September 20, 2007, quoted the US Census Bureau as saying that 47 million people in the United States were not covered by health insurance.

Racial Discrimination in the United States

Racial discrimination is a deep-rooted social illness in the United States, the report says.

Black people and other minor ethnic groups live in the bottom of the US society.

According to statistics released by the US Census Bureau in August 2007, median income of black households was 31,969 US dollars in 2006, or 61 percent of that for non-Hispanic white households. Median income for Hispanic households stood at 37,781 US dollars, 72 percent of that for non-Hispanic white households.

The rates of blacks and Hispanics living in poverty and without health insurance are much higher than non-Hispanic whites, according to *Washington Observer Weekly*.

Ethnic minorities have been subject to racial discrimination in employment and workplace. According to the US Department of Labor, in November 2007, the unemployment rate for black Americans was 8.4 percent, twice that of non-Hispanic whites (4.2 percent).

The unemployment rate for Hispanics was 5.7 percent. The jobless rates among blacks and Hispanics were much higher than that for non-Hispanic whites.

Racial discrimination in the US judicial system is shocking. According to the 2007 annual report on the state of black Americans issued by the National Urban League (NUL), African Americans (especially males) are more likely than whites to be convicted and sentenced to longer terms. Blacks are seven times more likely than whites to be incarcerated.

Women and Children in the United States

The report says the conditions of women and children in the United States are worrisome.

Women account for 51 percent of the US population, but there are only 86 women serving in the 110th US Congress. Women hold 16, or 16.0 percent of the 100 seats in the Senate and 70, or 16.1 percent of the 435 seats in the House of Representatives.

In December 2007, there were 76 women serving in state-wide elective executive offices, accounting for 24.1 percent of the total. The proportion of women in state legislature is 23.5 percent.

Discrimination against women is pervasive in US job market and workplaces. The US Equal Employment Opportunity Commission said it received 23,247 charges on sex-based discrimination in 2006, accounting for 30.7 percent of the total discrimination charges.

The living conditions of US children are of great concern. *Houston Chronicle* reported that a survey by the United Nations on 21 rich countries showed that though the United States was among the world's richest nations, its ranked only the 20th in the overall well-being of children.

US juveniles often fall victims of abuses and crimes. According to a report on school crimes in the United States released by the Department of Justice in December 2007, 57 out of one thousand US students above the age of 12 were victims of violence and property crimes in 2005.

Millions of underage girls become sex slaves in the United States. Statistics from the Department of Justice show some 100,000 to three million US children under the age of 18 are involved in prostitution. An FBI report says as high as 40 percent of forced prostitutes are minors.

How the United States Treats Other Countries

The report says the United States has a notorious record of trampling on the sovereignty of and violating human rights in other countries.

The invasion of Iraq by US troops has produced the biggest human rights tragedy and the greatest humanitarian disaster in the modern world. It was reported that since the invasion in 2003, 660,000 Iraqis have died, of which 99 percent were civilians. That translates into a daily toll of 450.

According to the *Los Angeles Times,* the number of civilian deaths in Iraq has exceeded one million. A report from the United Nations Children's Fund (UNICEF) revealed that about one million Iraqis were homeless, half of whom were children.

It is high time for the US government to face its own human rights problems with courage and give up the unwise practices of applying double standards on human rights issues, according to [a Chinese] report.

US troops have killed many innocent civilians in the anti-terrorism war in Afghanistan. The *Washington Post* reported on May 3, 2007, that as many as 51 civilians were killed by US soldiers in one week.

An Afghan human rights group said in a report that US Marine units fired indiscriminately at pedestrians, people in cars, buses and taxis along a 10-mile stretch of road in Nangarhar province on March 4, 2007, killing 12 civilians, including one infant and three elders.

It is high time for the US government to face its own human rights problems with courage and give up the unwise practices of applying double standards on human rights issues, according to the report.

This is the ninth consecutive year that the Information Office of the State Council has issued human rights record of the United States to answer the US State Department annual report.

Periodical and Internet Sources Bibliography

The following articles have been selected to supplement the diverse views presented in this chapter.

John Allen	"Governance Improves in Liberia, Angola, Togo but Declines in Eritrea, Madasgascar," allAfrica.com, October 4, 2010. http://allafrica.com.
Julius Barigaba	"Army Under Scrutiny for Rights Abuses in Karamoja," *East African* (Nairobi), October 11, 2010.
Peter Foster	"China Pledges to Human Rights—with Chinese Characteristics," *Telegraph* (UK), April 13, 2009.
Richard Goldstone	"International Justice: SA Leads the Way in Standing Up Against War Criminals," *Business-Day*, September 21, 2010.
Garry Leech	"Colombian Government's Role in Human Rights Abuses," *Colombia Journal*, May 8, 2009.
Charles Lewis	"By Putting Profit First, U.S. Turns 'Blind Eye' to Plight of Christians in China: Report," *National Post* (Canada), January 6, 2010.
Tom Marshall	"Migrant Abuse Widespread in Mexico, Local Groups Say," *Guadalajara Reporter*, September 10, 2010.
Colin Murphy	"Impunity in Guatemala," *Le Monde diplomatique* (Paris, France), December 15, 2009.
Tom Ndahiro	"Genocide Denial in Minds and Hearts," *New Times* (Rwanda), September 13, 2010.
Rajeshree Sisodia	"Nepal's Reform Stalls," *Le Monde diplomatique* (Paris, France), August 3, 2010.

GLOBALVIEWPOINTS

Human Rights and Politics

Britain's New Government Must Make Human Rights a Top Priority

Kate Allen

Kate Allen is the director of Amnesty International in the United Kingdom. In the following viewpoint, she urges Britain's new foreign secretary, William Hague, to pursue an agenda of human rights at home and abroad. Allen notes that Britain has a chance to establish global leadership on such issues and to be a force for good in the world.

As you read, consider the following questions:

1. What does the Amnesty International report on the global state of human rights say about the Taliban in Afghanistan?
2. What does the Foreign Office need to be apprised of if British personnel are again seized by the Iranian authorities, according to Allen?
3. Into what issues did William Hague announce an inquiry?

When the one-time foreign secretary Robin Cook became leader of the Commons in 2001 he famously "read himself into" his new role with a marathon 48-hour briefing ses-

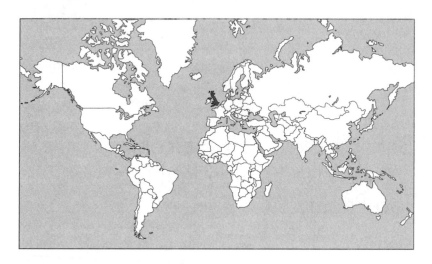

sion. As William Hague takes the measure of his new foreign secretary job, I urge him to steel himself for the challenges ahead with a little light reading: the new Amnesty International report 2010 (subtitled "The State of the World's Human Rights") published later this week.

Hague may not wish to devour our—often grim—400-page opus in one weekend, but here are some reasons why he should place it on a handy bookshelf in his office.

First, Hague will naturally be seeking to put numerous bilateral and multilateral relations on "reset". Starting with the United States, the UK is reestablishing where it stands on key issues, always, of course, assessed against the UK national interest. The tools for this reassessment are many and varied—economic and military data are key—but "softer" indices of judgement play a major role. This realm, broadly "political", must, I believe, include human rights if Britain is to make the right choices in the world.

Take Afghanistan, Hague's avowed priority issue. Equipment for troops, dealing with the narcotics trade, assessing already complex relations with Pakistan and Iran, the US and NATO—each of these will play a part in policy formation. But what of human rights in Afghanistan? We've been told numerous times that UK forces are in Afghanistan to stop terrorists killing people on the streets of Britain. Yet politicians have readily cited human rights concerns—especially virulent anti-women policies from the Taliban—as further cause and justification.

As Afghanistan prepares for the "Peace Jirga" on 29 May, the question is increasingly: On what terms does the Afghan government of Hamid Karzai attempt a peace settlement with the "reconcilable" elements of the Taliban and other armed groups? The US and NATO view on this will be important, so the UK must consider this extremely carefully.

Hague will read on page 55 of the Amnesty report that in 2009 the Taliban and other anti-government groups actually "stepped up attacks against civilians, including attacks on schools and health clinics, across the country". Worryingly enough, the report makes clear, Afghan women and girls were targeted for attack by the Taliban and were also the subject of widespread societal discrimination, forced marriage, domestic violence and other abuse.

The danger now, then, is that a rush to stem Taliban violence through a "peace" deal will mean women's already fragile rights being traded away. The UK should have no part in this "trade-off".

Other enormous challenges ahead require the same human rights input for any informed foreign policy thinking. Iran is far more than a "nuclear issue", as the huge election protest movement last year demonstrated. If, for example, British personnel are again seized by the Iranian authorities, the Foreign Office needs to be thoroughly apprised of detention conditions, the risk of torture, the fairness of trials and a host of other human rights issues. Indeed the same applies to all countries: There is no clearer example of British interests intersecting with those of the citizens of other countries as when a British national is detained in a foreign jail next to political prisoners in, say, Burma, China or Saudi Arabia.

Diplomacy is a two-way street. But no meeting with a foreign leader or their foreign affairs ministers should take place without the foreign secretary being less than fully aware of what occurs in the police stations of that country (in some instances in the basement cells of ministry buildings themselves). It's as well to know that the smiling prime minister's own brother is accused of torture if you're about to sign a multimillion-pound trade deal.

Certainly we can have no claim to the moral high ground unless our record is significantly better than it has been.

Meanwhile foreign powers are adept at seeing the beam in our own eye if we broach their human rights failings. Getting our human rights house in order makes good sense internationally and domestically. The unpleasant fact is that the UK's involvement in "war on terror" secret detentions and torture left us exposed to justified criticism. Hague's announcement last week that there would be an inquiry into this is overdue but extremely welcome. Certainly we can have no claim to the moral high ground unless our record is significantly better than it has been.

The UK can be a force for good in the world in multiple ways—from firm support for the UN millennium development goals and an effective International Criminal Court, to continued championing of a global arms trade treaty and of lifesaving measures on maternal health and HIV/AIDS treatments. In a speech to FCO staff on his first day in the job, Hague mentioned the importance of "international organisations", a promising enough sign that we'll be monitoring here in terms of support for human rights at the United Nations, the EU and elsewhere.

Hague and his Conservative-Lib Dem coalition colleagues have an opportunity to pursue an agenda of law, order and human rights at home and abroad. A well-informed, human rights–aware Foreign Office is a boon to good government and much will rest on the decisions taken in the first years of the new foreign secretary's tenure. As well as absorbing his FCO briefs, William Hague should read our report in full. I've already mailed him a copy.

Myanmar's Government Must Be Pressured to Hold Fair Elections

U Win Tin

U Win Tin is a member of the central executive committee and a founder of the National League for Democracy (NLD) party in Myanmar (officially the Republic of the Union of Myanmar, also known as Burma). In the following viewpoint, he describes the systematic repression of the NLD by the military regime governing Myanmar through restrictive election laws, imprisonment of political dissidents and opponents, and violence. Tin urges the Association of Southeast Asian Nations (ASEAN) to pressure Myanmar's government to finally hold fair elections and to respect the will of the people.

As you read, consider the following questions:

1. How does the new election law in Myanmar sideline the National League for Democracy (NLD)?
2. What will happen if the military's elections go ahead without the participation of key parties and are accepted by the international community, according to the author?
3. What should the Association of Southeast Asian Nations (ASEAN) do to help Myanmar?

U Win Tin, "Myanmar's Prison of an Election Will Also Be ASEAN's," *Jakarta Post*, May 27, 2010. Reprinted by permission.

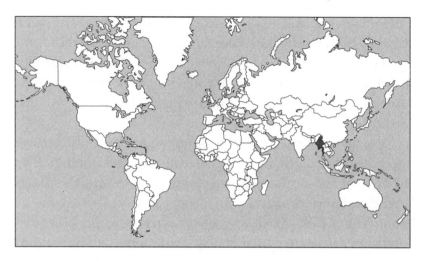

In Myanmar's last elections, twenty years ago today [May 27, 2010], the people of Myanmar [officially the Republic of the Union of Myanmar, also known as Burma] voted for a democratic change by overwhelmingly electing the National League for Democracy (NLD). However, the people's desire was never honored.

Ever since the military regime lost in the 1990 elections, they have been trying to violently sideline the NLD.

The most recent evidence of this is the issuing of highly restrictive election laws, requiring political parties, including the NLD, to cast out members imprisoned as political prisoners and pledge to abide by the deeply flawed 2008 constitution.

NLD Has No Options

These election laws have left us, the NLD, with no principled or practical options but to refuse to participate in the elections. Other 1990 election-winning ethnic political parties have made the same decision.

If the military's elections go ahead without the participation of key parties and are accepted by the international community, the military rule will be further entrenched and stand in the way of ASEAN's [Association of Southeast Asian Nations'] goals of regional peace, stability, and progress.

When the NLD began campaigning for the 1990 elections in Myanmar, our members throughout the country saw the immense physical suffering and widespread discontent that existed everywhere.

People were hungry for freedom and democratic change after decades of living under a military dictatorship. The NLD's triumph in the polls—winning over 82 percent of seats in the parliament—was a strong sign that people trusted Daw Aung San Suu Kyi [former general secretary of the NLD and controversial winner of the 1990 prime ministerial election] and the NLD to help bring positive change to their country.

The NLD wanted to create a new constitution and a new Myanmar that respected the rights of all people, through co-operation and trust building. Though we were denied our rightful positions in the government, we have continuously worked towards these goals and will do the same even now that we have been outlawed by the regime.

We have repeatedly extended our hand to the military regime asking for the inclusive dialogue needed to move towards national reconciliation, only to be rejected time and time again.

Attempts at Reconciliation

We have repeatedly extended our hand to the military regime asking for the inclusive dialogue needed to move towards national reconciliation, only to be rejected time and time again. We were barred from participating in their sham "Roadmap to Democracy," including the writing of the 2008 constitution.

With the announcement of new election laws, the regime officially annulled the results of the 1990 elections and our landslide victory claiming, "the result does not conform with the [2008] constitution".

Association of Southeast Asian Nations (ASEAN) Member Countries

The ASEAN aims to promote regional peace and collaboration, as well as economic growth, social progress, and cultural development.

TAKEN FROM: ASEAN Secretariat, 2009. *www.aseansec.org.*

However, the constitution itself does not conform with the will of the people as well as international standards. Forcibly ratified in the wake of [tropical storm] Cyclone Nargis, the constitution guarantees continued military control, ethnic repression and restricts political freedom.

A Controversial Decision

The NLD's decision to not participate in the election has been quite controversial. Some people in the international community see these elections as a hopeful step forward. However, it is clear to us that they will not improve the lives of the people of Myanmar. We cannot participate in elections that go against the very principles of democracy, rule of law, human rights for which thousands of people have sacrificed their lives.

Moreover, we cannot participate for several practical reasons. The regime continues to deny ethnic communities—over 30 percent of Myanmar's population—equal rights and self-determination resulting in ongoing armed conflict, more refugees and increased instability.

Many ethnic communities and armed groups are opposing the elections unless their demands for ethnic equality are met. They have supported Daw Aung San Suu Kyi and the urgent need for genuine political dialogue, and we will not turn our backs on their demands.

These elections will also not ease the dire poverty that the majority of people in Myanmar face. The economy will still be under the control of the hands of the military regime and its cronies, driven by their personal gains rather than the needs of the people.

What ASEAN Should Do

Despite the tremendous flaws with the upcoming elections, there has been a noticeable and troubling silence from ASEAN. ASEAN must recognize that what happens in Myanmar will affect the entire region.

ASEAN is working towards greater integration by 2015. However, if the elections proceed according to the regime's plans, ASEAN will be aligning themselves with an unstable country that stands on false democratic methods and restricting their own progress.

ASEAN Secretary-General Surin Pitsuwan has excused ASEAN's inaction by stating that ASEAN is "not a magic wand that can deliver a miracle in every issue." ASEAN may not be a "magic wand", but it is certainly poised to have the greatest geostrategic influence on the behavior of its most unruly member.

Finding the Right Solutions

ASEAN has significant political leverage on Myanmar and must pressure the regime to finally take the necessary steps towards national reconciliation: release all political prisoners including Daw Aung San Suu Kyi, cease attacks against ethnic communities, and engage in inclusive dialogue with democratic and ethnic representatives. ASEAN can no longer hide behind its policy of noninterference, allowing tyranny to continue beyond these elections.

The NLD is committed to finding the right solutions for Myanmar. We made the decision to not participate because it is what is right and what is needed.

I implore ASEAN and the international community to do the same by calling on the regime to take steps towards national reconciliation and genuine democracy, and refuse to recognize the results of these elections if they fail to do so.

China Must Stop Supporting Authoritarian Regimes

Martin Walker

Martin Walker is editor emeritus of United Press International (UPI). In the following viewpoint, Walker discusses China's role in supporting five authoritarian regimes. China's support for authoritarian regimes begins with its own ruthless handling of the protests in Tibet. China gives diplomatic protection to Myanmar and Sudan in the United Nations (UN) and makes deals with the government of Uzbekistan in defiance of UN efforts to condemn the repression of protests there. In both Sudan and Uzbekistan, Chinese oil interests appear to be at stake. North Korea is virtually dependent on China and gave military support to Zimbabwe's president, Robert Mugabe, during his attack on the Matabele tribes of his rival when Mugabe was consolidating his power after the conflict for independence. China's policy of keeping internal matters under its own sovereignty and its growing strength as an economic power contribute to weakening the effectiveness of international opinion in influencing China to recognize the human rights of its own citizens and of the people in the countries with which it does business.

As you read, consider the following questions:

1. What is the name of China's current leader, and what role did he play in the Tibetan unrest in 1989–1990?

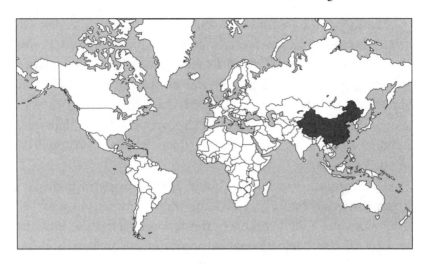

2. According to the author, what are some signs of Chinese support for Myanmar besides protection in the United Nations?

3. Who is Islam Karimov, and what is his relationship to China?

Washington, March 17 (UPI)—One sobering aspect of the tragedy of Tibet is to consider a list of the places in the world where abuses of human rights are most common. Darfur in Sudan, Zimbabwe, North Korea, Myanmar (or Burma), Uzbekistan and Tibet would come high on most people's lists.

And what they have in common is the crucial enabling role of China. Tibet, where the official Chinese figure of 10 dead in the disturbances of the last four days is dwarfed by the more reliable reports from inside the country of more than 100 dead, has been under direct Chinese rule since 1951.

Tibet has been ruled with an iron hand, while also being colonized by the deliberate immigration of vast numbers of Han Chinese as part of what the Dalai Lama calls "cultural genocide." Han Chinese shopkeepers have been a particular target of the latest riots.

It should not be forgotten that China's current leader, Hu Jintao, boasts in his credentials for high office his ruthless role in crushing the last round of Tibetan unrest in 1989–90, when he was party chief in Lhasa. It was an unruly time, following the death of the Panchen Lama, an important Buddhist religious leader (and may Tibetan exiles suspect Hu of having a hand in his passing) and the award of the Nobel Peace Prize to the Dalai Lama.

Hu imposed martial law, sent 2,000 troops into the Tibetan districts of Lhasa, and somewhere between 40 and 120 Tibetans were killed. Many hundreds were arrested, and the reports of the U.N. Special Rapporteur on Torture contain heartrending accounts of their fate.

As a reward for his ruthlessness, Hu was then promoted by Jiang Zemin to the standing committee of the Communist Party's Central Committee, making him in effect the leading heir for the eventual top job. Tibetan exiles say Hu clambered to supreme power over Tibetan corpses.

Hu imposed martial law, sent 2,000 troops into the Tibetan districts of Lhasa, and somewhere between 40 and 120 Tibetans were killed.

China's role elsewhere is less direct, but equally unsavory. North Korea is close to being a Chinese client state, largely dependent on the oil pipeline from China. Myanmar, where the ruthless suppression of the protests by Buddhist monks earlier this year now looks like a grisly dress rehearsal of the events in Tibet, has Chinese military and electronic eavesdropping posts on its islands, Chinese engineers building ports, roads and oil and gas terminals, and Chinese diplomatic protection in the United Nations.

China also rides shotgun in the United Nations for Sudan, which provides 10 percent of China's oil imports. In Sudan and Myanmar alike, China's oil interests appear to trump the

The China–North Korea Relationship

China has supported North Korea ever since Chinese fighters flooded onto the Korean peninsula to fight for their comrades in the Democratic People's Republic of Korea (DPRK) in 1950. Since the Korean War divided the peninsula between the North and South, China has lent political and economic backing to North Korea's leaders: Kim Il-sung and his son and successor, Kim Jong-il.

In recent years, China has been one of the authoritarian regime's few allies. But this long-standing relationship suffered a strain when Pyongyang [the capital of North Korea] tested a nuclear weapon in October 2006 and China agreed to UN [United Nations] Security Council Resolution 1718, which imposed sanctions on Pyongyang.

Jayshree Bajoria,
"The China-North Korea Relationship,"
Council on Foreign Relations, July 21, 2009.

desire of some Chinese diplomats to play a rather more responsible role in international affairs.

China has also helped to prop up the wretched regime of Zimbabwe's President Robert Mugabe. It has had considerable backing from China's North Korean crony, whose military "advisers" infamously helped Mugabe crush the Matabele tribes of the south in the early 1980s to consolidate his rule. Estimates of the death toll range from 3,000 to 7,000.

China also turned a blind eye to the massacres of protesters two years ago in the Uzbekistan cities of Andijan and Pahktaabad. Official figures say 169 died, but eyewitness reports claimed more than 700 dead. Shortly afterward, Uzbek President Islam Karimov was honored in Beijing by Hu as "an old friend of the Chinese people."

Karimov then signed a $600 million oil exploration agreement with China, which in effect broke U.N. efforts to rally an international condemnation of the Uzbek repression.

"As to what has happened recently in Uzbekistan, it is the internal affairs of the country," said China's Foreign Ministry spokesman. "We have all along firmly supported the efforts of the Uzbek Government to fight the three forces of terrorists, separatists and extremists."

As an authoritarian regime with little regard for the human rights of its own people, nor to their free access to information, China insists other countries have no right to interfere in the internal affairs of sovereign states. At the same time, there are signs that China is open to reform, most notably in its limited cooperation in the six-nation process for dealing with the North Korean nuclear issue.

Even before the United States slid into recession, China's ownership of some $1.5 trillion in U.S. Treasury bills, dollars and foreign exchange gave Beijing enormous international leverage.

But the bottom line is that China is almost impervious to international influence, and it knows it. Even before the United States slid into recession, China's ownership of some $1.5 trillion in U.S. Treasury bills, dollars and foreign exchange gave Beijing enormous international leverage. And now that China's own growth rate may be the last thing stopping the global economy from following the United States into recession, there is little appetite for challenging China over Tibet.

The Tibetan crisis was predictable. Tibetan activists, and Uighur Muslim activists in western China, know that this year's Beijing Olympic Games gave them an opportunity. Beijing knew that the Games could make it vulnerable to disturbances and that repression would attract a large and critical international audience.

In its efficient way, Beijing has doubtless prepared for trouble and carefully worked out its most effective and least damaging response. Given its economic weight in world affairs, China has probably calculated that its image and its Games will not suffer unduly from its repression in Tibet or its accommodating way with dictators.

If they are right, then the rallying cry of human rights that proved surprisingly effective when applied to the old Soviet Union may be losing its force. This would be a dismaying loss. Human rights have given the United Nations, the United States, Europe and much of the rest of the world a cause to which they can rally, or at least pay lip service.

It may be one of those hypocrisies by which vice pays tribute to virtue, but the iconic role of human rights since the Helsinki treaties of 1975 has been one of the most promising developments in international affairs. If China continues to get away with flouting the elementary rights of the U.N. Charter, we shall all be the losers.

Israel Violates Human Rights and the European Union Is Complicit

Badriya Khan

Badriya Khan is a political analyst. In the following viewpoint, Khan reports that an international tribunal, the Russell Tribunal on Palestine (RTP), has found that Israel has violated international law and the European Union (EU) is complicit. It is recommended that the EU refrain from contributing to Israel's lawbreaking and the subsequent oppression of the Palestinian people.

As you read, consider the following questions:

1. Who set up the Russell Tribunal?
2. According to the RTP, how has Israel violated international law?
3. How does the RTP argue that the EU should treat Israel?

Things are worsening for Israel from moral and legal perspectives. In fact, one year after the Goldstone report on its 'war crimes' during its war on Gaza and amidst growing suspicions of its direct responsibility in the assassination of a Palestinian leader in Dubai, an international court has now concluded that Israel is violating international' law with Europe's complicity.

Badriya Khan, "Israel Violates International Law with EU Complicity," Global Research.ca, March 5, 2010. Reprinted by permission of IDN-InDepthNews, Globalom Media.

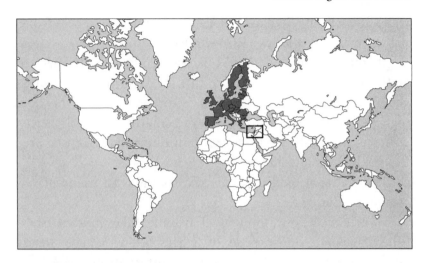

The European Union (EU) is an accomplice of Israel in its proven violations of international law, as it legitimised Israeli actions in the Palestinian occupied territories and provided support to it, according to the findings of the Russell Tribunal on Palestine (RTP), which met in Barcelona on March 1–3 [2010].

The tribunal concluded that Israel has committed and continues to commit violations of international law, while the EU and its member states have breached this law and failed to take measures against Israeli violations and identify remedies.

The RTP, which was set up by late British philosopher, mathematician, historian, pacifist and social critic Bertrand Russell to judge the Vietnam War from the perspective of international law, has also stated that "Israel practices a systematic policy of discrimination with the Palestinian population by closing Gaza's borders and limiting the movement of people across the territory."

The RTP is an international citizen-based "Tribunal of conscience" created in response to the demands of civil society. It is imbued with the same spirit and espouses the same rigorous rules as those inherited from the tribunal by Bertrand Russell on Vietnam (1966–1967) and the Russell Tribunal II on Latin America (1974–1976).

Its members include Nobel laureates, a former UN [United Nations] secretary-general, a former UN undersecretary-general, two former heads of state, other persons who held high political office and many representatives of civil society, writers, journalists, poets, actors, film directors, scientists, professors, lawyers and judges.

International public law constitutes the legal frame of reference for the RTP.

In its conclusions, the Russell Tribunal takes it as an established fact that some aspects of Israel's behavior have already been characterized as violations of international law by a number of international bodies, including the UN Security Council, the General Assembly and the International Court of Justice (ICJ).

The European Union (EU) is an accomplice of Israel in its proven violations of international law, as it legitimised Israeli actions in the Palestinian occupied territories and provided support to it.

Israel's Violations of International Law

Having taken note of reports and heard witnesses, the RTP finds that "Israel has committed and continues to commit grave breaches of international law against the Palestinian people."

According to the RTP, Israel violates international law:

By maintaining a form of domination and subjugation over the Palestinians that prevents them from freely determining their political status, Israel violates the right of the Palestinian people to self-determination inasmuch as it is unable to exercise its sovereignty on the territory which belongs to it.

This violates the declaration on the granting of independence to colonial countries and peoples and all UN General

Assembly [UNGA] resolutions that have reaffirmed the right of the Palestinian people to self-determination since 1969.

By occupying Palestinian territories since June 1967 and refusing to leave them, Israel violates the Security Council resolutions that demand its withdrawal from those territories.

By pursuing a policy of systematic discrimination against Palestinians in Israeli territory or in the occupied territories, Israel commits acts that may be characterised as apartheid; these acts include:

- the closure of the borders of the Gaza Strip and restrictions on the freedom of movement of its inhabitants;

- the prevention of the return of Palestinian refugees to their home or land of origin;

- the prohibition on the free use by Palestinians of certain natural resources such as the watercourses within their land.

"Given the discriminatory nature of these measures, since they are based, inter alia, on the nationality of the persons to whom they are applied, the RTP finds that they present features comparable to apartheid, even though they do not emanate from an identical political regime to that prevailing in South Africa prior to 1994".

By constructing a Wall in the West Bank on Palestinian territory that it occupies, Israel denies the Palestinians access to their own land, violates their property rights and seriously restricts the freedom of movement.

Criminal Acts of Apartheid

The tribunal concludes that these measures are characterised as "criminal acts" by the [International] Convention on the Suppression and Punishment of the Crime of Apartheid of

July 18, 1976, "which is not in fact binding on Israel, though this does not exonerate Israel in that regard". In particular:

By annexing Jerusalem in July 1980 and maintaining the annexation, Israel violates the prohibition of the acquisition of territory by force, as stated by the Security Council.

By constructing a Wall in the West Bank on Palestinian territory that it occupies, Israel denies the Palestinians access to their own land, violates their property rights and seriously restricts the freedom of movement of the Palestinian population, thereby violating article 12 of the International Covenant on Civil and Political Rights to which Israel has been a party since 3 October 1991.

The illegality of the construction of the Wall was confirmed by the ICJ in its advisory opinion of July 9, 2004, which was endorsed by the UNGA in its resolution ES-10/15.

By systematically building settlements in Jerusalem and the West Bank, Israel breaches the rules of international humanitarian law governing occupation, in particular article 49 of the Fourth Geneva Convention of 12 August 1949, by which Israel has been bound since 6 July 1951. This point was noted by the ICJ.

By pursuing a policy of targeted killings against Palestinians whom it describes as "terrorists" without first attempting to arrest them, Israel violates the right to life of the persons concerned, a right enshrined in article 6 of the [International] Covenant on Civil and Political Rights.

By maintaining a blockade on the Gaza Strip in breach of the provisions of the Fourth Geneva Convention of 12 August 1949 (art. 33), which prohibits collective punishment.

By inflicting extensive and serious damage, especially on persons and civilian property, and by using prohibited methods of combat during Operation Cast Lead in Gaza (December 2008–January 2009).

Palestinian Loss of Land, 1946 to 2000

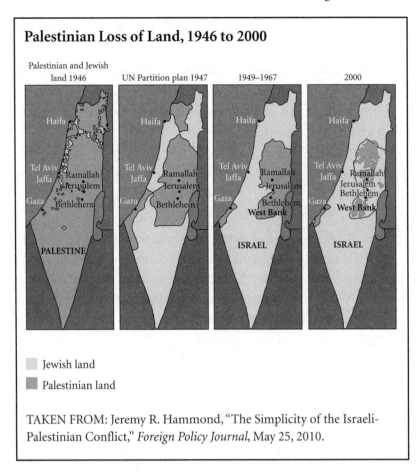

Palestinian and Jewish
land 1946 · UN Partition plan 1947 · 1949–1967 · 2000

Jewish land

Palestinian land

TAKEN FROM: Jeremy R. Hammond, "The Simplicity of the Israeli-Palestinian Conflict," *Foreign Policy Journal*, May 25, 2010.

EU Violations, Direct and Indirect

While the EU and its member states are not the direct perpetrators of these acts, "they nevertheless violate international law and the internal legal order of the EU as set down in the EU treaty either by failing to take the measures that Israel's conduct requires them to take or by contributing directly or indirectly to such conduct," underlines the RTP.

It adds that Israel's violations of international law are frequently violations of "peremptory norms" of international law: targeted killings that violate the right to life, deprivation of the liberty of Palestinians in conditions that violate the prohibition of torture, violation of the right of peoples to self-determination, living conditions imposed on a people that constitute a type of "apartheid."

"The EU and its member states are therefore under an obligation to react in application of international law to prevent violations of peremptory norms of international law and to counteract their consequences," concludes the tribunal.

"By failing to take appropriate action to that end, the EU and its member states are breaching an elementary obligation of due diligence pertaining to respect for the most fundamental rules of international law."

The RTP considered that this obligation to react implies, in accordance with the rules of good faith and due diligence, the obligation to ensure that the reaction against violations of peremptory norms of international law complies with the principle of reasonable effectiveness.

"To that end, the EU and its member states must use all available legal channels to ensure that Israel respects international law. It therefore calls for a response that goes beyond mere declarations condemning the breaches of international law committed by Israel."

Of course, the RTP takes note of these declarations, "but they are no more than a first step when it comes to meeting the international obligations of the EU and its member states; they are not fully performing the duty of reaction imposed by the rules of international law."

Lastly, the RTP emphasised that the obligation to react against violations of peremptory norms of international law must be subject to a rule of nondiscrimination and of unacceptability of double standards.

"The RTP is perfectly well aware that states have not codified a rule of equidistance in respect of the obligation to react, but it holds that such a rule is inferable as a matter of course from the principles of good faith and reasonable interpretation of international law: Refusing to accept it will inevitably lead to 'a result which is manifestly absurd or unreasonable' and which is ruled out by treaty law".

EU Discrimination and Complicity

In these circumstances, "the RTP considered that it is unacceptable and contrary to the aforementioned juridical logic for the EU to suspend its relations, de facto, with Palestine when Hamas [an Islamic resistance movement] was elected in the occupied Palestinian territories and to maintain them with a state that violates international law on a far greater scale than Hamas."

Regarding the failure by the EU and its member states "to refrain from contributing to the violations of international law committed by Israel", the RTP noted that "reports by experts have brought to light passive and active forms of assistance by the EU and its member states for violations of international law by Israel."

For these acts to qualify as "unlawful assistance or aid to Israel", two conditions must be met: The state providing assistance must do so with the intention of facilitating the wrongful act attributable to Israel and it must do so knowingly, according to the RTP.

The RTP explains that the EU and its member states could not have been unaware that some forms of assistance to Israel contributed or would perforce contribute to certain wrongful acts committed by Israel. This is applicable to:

- exports of military equipment to a state that has maintained an illegal occupation for more than forty years;

- imports of produce from settlements located in occupied territories and no real control by the customs authorities of EU member states of the origin of such produce;

- evidence of a report repressed in 2005 and repeated internal reports by EU officials to EU bodies listing violations accurately, only to be ignored by those bodies.

In both cases, this conduct "contributed significantly to the wrongful acts committed by Israel" even if they did not directly cause such acts, and it is reasonable to assume that the EU could not possibly have been unaware of this.

"In these cases, the EU may be held to have been complicit in the wrongful act committed by Israel and hence to incur responsibility," the tribunal emphasised.

The EU's Proactive Silence in Support of Israeli Action

Moreover, the participation of Israeli settlements in European research programmes, the failure of the EU to complain during the "Cast Lead" operation about the destruction by Israel of infrastructure that the EU had funded in Gaza, and the (proposed) upgrading of bilateral relations between the EU and Israel, it stressed, are characterised by a number of experts as assistance to Israel in its alleged violations of international law.

Even if the acts of the EU and its member states do not contribute directly to Israeli violations of international law, "they provide a form of security for Israel's policy and encourage it to violate international law because they cast the EU and its member states in the role of approving spectators."

"The silence of the EU and its member states seems like tacit approval or a sign of acceptance of violations of international law by Israel," the Russell Tribunal judged.

"As it is inconceivable that the EU and its member states are unaware of the violations of international law being committed by Israel," the RTP concludes that the acts in question constitute wrongful assistance to Israel within the meaning of aforementioned article 16 of the UN International Law Commission draft articles on state responsibility.

North Korea Must Shut Down Its Concentration Camps

Lee Jong-Heon

Lee Jong-Heon is a correspondent for United Press International (UPI). In the following viewpoint, Jong-Heon describes the conditions in concentration camps in North Korea. According to the testimony of defectors from North Korea, including dozens of gulag escapees, North Korea holds an estimated two hundred thousand prisoners in six camps across the country. The camps are used as a key tool to suppress potential dissidents and to tame famine-hit people by spreading a sense of fear. Most of the camps are considered Total Control Zones, and a sentence to one of these camps constitutes a life sentence filled with forced labor from 5 A.M. to 9:30 P.M. every day, a poor diet, and no medical care under fear of torture, rape, and execution. According to Shin Dong-hyuk, the first escapee from such a zone, some inmates such as himself were born in the camps. His father, as a reward for good work in the camp, was allowed to marry a female inmate. Children born in the camp remain in the camp. At the age of fourteen, Shin and his father were forced to watch the public execution of his mother and brother after a failed escape attempt. Some North Korean defectors and civic activists in

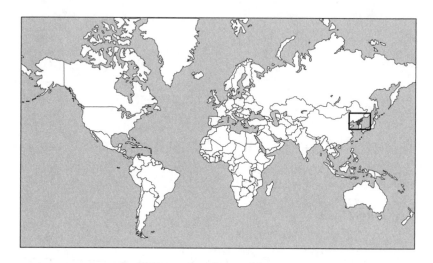

Seoul have filed a petition with the International Criminal Court in The Hague, calling for a probe into the North's alleged human rights violations and for North Korea's dictator Kim Jong-il to be put on trial.

As you read, consider the following questions:

1. Who is Lee Myung-bak, and what is his role in the story of the North Korean concentration camps?

2. What percentage of the total population is estimated to be imprisoned in these camps, according to the viewpoint?

3. For what offenses could a prisoner be executed, according to the viewpoint?

Seoul, South Korea—North Korea runs six large prison camps for political prisoners that together hold an estimated 200,000 inmates and are used as a key tool to suppress potential dissidents and tame famine-hit people by spreading a sense of fear, South Korea's state-run human rights watchdog said on Wednesday.

The report of the National Human Rights Commission is the first formal document on North Korea's gulags made by South Korea's government or state agencies.

The liberal governments that ruled South Korea for the past decade had a policy of inter-Korean reconciliation, and maintained a low-key stance toward human rights abuses in the North for fear of creating friction with Pyongyang and upsetting the fragile cross-border reconciliation process.

But South Korean President Lee Myung-bak, who took office in early 2008 as the country's first conservative leader in a decade, has vowed to speak out against human rights violations in the North, saying that the human rights issue is "something we cannot avoid" and North Korea "should know it."

Under Lee's policy, for the first time the watchdog has conducted investigations into alleged human rights abuses in North Korea, mostly by interviewing defectors from the North.

Most of the camps are designated "Total Control Zones" that house "enemies of the people" deemed incorrigible.

The watchdog's report, "Conditions on Political Prison Camps in North Korea," is based on the testimonies of 371 defectors, including dozens of gulag escapees.

"An estimated 200,000 political prisoners have been incarcerated in six camps across North Korea," the report said. The figure is equal to around 1 percent of the country's total population. "The inmates are suffering starvation, torture, forced labor, rape and executions out of global attention," the report said.

Most of the camps are designated "Total Control Zones" that house "enemies of the people" deemed incorrigible. The other camps are "Revolutionizing Zones" and house those considered less threatening to the totalitarian regime.

"All of the camps except No. 18 Camp and a small part of No. 15 Camp are designated as Total Control Zones," the report said. "Once sent to the zone, it is a life sentence," it said.

Little is known in the outside world about the Total Control Zones. According to Shin Dong-hyuk, the first escapee from such a zone, the camp where he lived was totally isolated from the outside world. "Inmates accepted hardships as a fact of life. We had no complaints about the hardships in the camp," he said in a recent testimony.

Shin had been an inmate all his life since he was born in 1982 at Camp No. 14 in Kaechon, north of Pyongyang, one of the Total Control Zones, until his dramatic escape in January 2005.

Shin's father had been sent to the camp in 1965 after his two brothers had defected to South Korea. As a reward for good work, the father was allowed to marry a female inmate who gave birth to Shin and his elder brother.

At the age of 14, Shin and his father were forced to sit in the first row to watch the public execution of his mother and brother. His mother was hanged while his brother was shot due to a failed escape attempt. Shin's father was severely beaten and tortured for the family's "anti-nation crime," which referred to the escape attempt.

Inmates of the camp were forced, he said, to monitor each other and report any "strange" behavior. They were not allowed to get together with more than three people or to move outside their worksites. "If they violated the rules, anybody was subject to execution," he said.

Shin also said that inmates were forced to toil from 5 A.M. to 9:30 P.M. every day, were fed a poor diet and were not provided any medical care. "Anyone who failed to achieve work quotas could be executed because it was considered as an expression of discontent," he said.

The human rights watchdog also said that the North has imposed much harsher punishments on citizens who tried to flee the country since 2008. An increasing number of North

South Korea's "Sunshine Policy"

South Koreans want reunification with the North [Korea], but not right away, polls show. . . . They worry about political collapse in the impoverished North and are afraid that dealing with it would lower their living standards, according to government officials and independent analysts.

For most of the past decade, South Korea's official "Sunshine Policy" toward the North was all but silent on human rights issues. . . .

[South Korean President Lee Myung-bak's] government, which took power in February [2008], has taken a harder line with North Korea, but . . . the public remains reluctant to condition assistance on issues such as prison camps, slave labor and torture.

Blaine Harden,
"Escapee Tells of Horrors in North Korean Prison Camp,"
Washington Post, *December 11, 2008.*

Koreans have crossed the border into China in recent years. Some have succeeded in reaching South Korea, although most are hiding in China or in neighboring countries.

The report comes at a time when South Korea and the United States have stepped up challenges to North Korea over its human rights record, and could provide food aid if Pyongyang returns to international nuclear talks.

The U.S. special envoy for North Korean human rights, Robert King, who travelled to Seoul last week, described conditions in the reclusive country as "appalling." On his first trip overseas since being confirmed by the U.S. Senate last November, King blasted the North as "one of the worst places in terms of the lack of human rights."

The U.N. special rapporteur on North Korean human rights, Vitit Muntarbhorn, also visited South Korea last week to gather information on conditions in the North and meet defectors and human rights activists.

An increasing number of North Koreans have crossed the border into China in recent years. Some have succeeded in reaching South Korea, although most are hiding in China or in neighboring countries.

In December, Robert Park, a 28-year-old Korean American from Arizona, slipped into the North to call for the regime to release political prisoners, shut concentration camps and improve human rights conditions.

A group of civic activists and North Korean defectors in Seoul have filed a petition with the International Criminal Court in The Hague, calling for a probe into the North's alleged human rights violations, including extreme torture, sexual slavery and prison brutality. They have also urged the court to put the North's dictator Kim Jong-il on trial.

"We were subjected to reduced food rations so extreme that we literally saw scores of our fellow prisoners die of malnutrition, starvation and disease," the group said in their petition.

The letter has also been sent to U.N. Secretary-General Ban Ki-moon and the U.N. High Commissioner for Refugees.

The European Union Should Support Democracy and Human Rights in Turkmenistan and Uzbekistan

Jos Boonstra

Jos Boonstra is a senior researcher at FRIDE, an international think tank based in Madrid that focuses on issues of security, human rights, and promoting democracy. In the following viewpoint, Boonstra argues that the European Union (EU) should strengthen its ties with Turkmenistan and Uzbekistan to encourage them to improve their records on human rights.

As you read, consider the following questions:

1. What is Uzbekistan's ruler Islam Karimov's record on human rights, according to the report?

2. How does the report classify NATO's role in Turkmenistan and Uzbekistan?

3. How does the United States want the Organization for Security and Co-operation in Europe (OSCE) to function in Turkmenistan and Uzbekistan, according to Boonstra?

Jos Boonstra "Defending Human Rights and Promoting Democracy: Euro-Atlantic Approaches Towards Turkmenistan and Uzbekistan," FRIDE Activity Brief, December 12, 2008, pp. 2–4. Reprinted by permission.

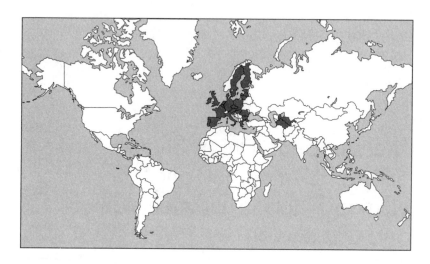

Turkmenistan witnessed a swift change of leadership when Gurbanguly Berdimuhamedow took over from absolute ruler Saparmurat Niyazov, who died at the end of 2006. Whereas some progress was made in terms of legislative reform and opening the country up to the outside world, hopes for an overhaul of the administration and engagement with political reform seem to have evaporated.

The majority of changes and reforms that have taken place over the last two years [2006–2008] have been cosmetic. President Berdimuhamedow wants to be seen as a reformer but, at the same time, he is carefully building up his own power base that might turn into a new personality cult.

The country remains isolated but tries to build relations with the EU [European Union], especially in the energy sector. The quantity of Turkmen gas deposits is uncertain and the regime wants to settle big contracts as soon as possible. Meanwhile, it remains very difficult to do business in and with Turkmenistan in other economic sectors.

There is no reason for the EU or its member states to be hesitant in criticising the enormous human rights violations that take place in Turkmenistan. A more active and critical stance would be welcomed and would not be likely to isolate

Turkmenistan further. In this sense, the EU could look to the US, a country that is critical in its dealings with [Turkmenistan's capital] Ashgabat.

In working with Turkmenistan, the EU might want to make use of countries that often have identical interests and are better positioned to work with Ashgabat, such as Kazakhstan, Russia and Turkey.

There is no reason for the EU or its member states to be hesitant in criticising the enormous human rights violations that take place in Turkmenistan.

Uzbekistan's Poor Human Rights Record

Uzbekistan is ruled by Islam Karimov, who has not shown any willingness to engage in democratic reform and has failed to improve the poor human rights record he gained in May 2005, when Uzbek security forces killed hundreds of protesters in the city of Andijon. When Uzbek authorities proved unwilling to allow international organisations to investigate these tragic events, the EU and the US imposed sanctions. As a result, Uzbekistan has turned to Russia, which largely abstained from criticising it, and has moved away from Western countries. This scenario is currently changing as the United States and the EU, headed by German initiatives, seek to repair ties with [Uzbekistan's capital] Tashkent.

Uzbekistan represents a threat to regional security due to its instability. There seems to be no post-Karimov scenario, while unrest and frustration is mounting in the most populous Central Asian country. The growth of radical Islam might prove to be another factor that could increase instability.

Uzbekistan has engaged with the EU in a human rights dialogue and has organised a civil society seminar jointly with the EU on media freedom. Unfortunately, only pro-regime NGOs [nongovernmental organisations] were invited to this seminar.

The human rights situation has barely improved, despite EU sanctions upon Tashkent leaders' travels to Europe and a weapons embargo (the latter is still in place). The Uzbek leadership has acquired a skill in making cosmetic changes in order to satisfy important partners: It did so in 2001–2, when the US needed access to Uzbekistan for the war on terrorism in Afghanistan; and it has done so in relation to the EU over the past year [2008]. Nonetheless, some positive movement is noticeable in local legislation. How this relates to practice is yet to be seen.

Human rights abuses, such as forced child labour in cotton fields, remain one of the most visible offences in Uzbekistan.

The EU Strategy for Central Asia

In June 2007, the European Union presented a strategy for Central Asia. Since then, the Union has been strengthening a regional approach towards the area, focusing especially on bilateral ties with Central Asian republics. Brussels [Belgium, the capital of the European Union] has concluded 'bilateral priority papers' with Turkmenistan and Uzbekistan, but has also established human rights dialogues with Ashgabat and Tashkent. Human rights, the rule of law, good governance and democratisation constitute the first priority outlined in the Strategy for Central Asia, though the EU has to balance this interest with an engagement on security and energy.

Human rights dialogues have now taken place in all five Central Asian countries. The EU touches upon a range of human rights questions with the Central Asian authorities, from media freedom and child protection, to freedom of assembly and women's rights. Kazakhstan and Kyrgyzstan objected to the dialogues because they feel their standards are higher than those of Turkmenistan and Uzbekistan. The Turkmen and Uzbek leaderships welcome these dialogues, provided they are held behind closed doors.

The EU has come a long way in a short time in terms of upgrading its relations with the countries of Central Asia. This is part of an ongoing process and Spain can play an important role in upgrading and strengthening the EU strategy for Central Asia. Indeed, building an effective and broad engagement will ultimately require the interest and actions of a broad range of member states.

EU moves to strengthen its role in Central Asia should take into account the experience of other organisations and countries that have been active in the region for longer. A broad lesson from these other approaches is, in particular, the need for a clear political vision for the region to guide engagement and to avoid projects becoming the driving force of relations. This is especially important for the difficult cases of Uzbekistan and Turkmenistan. The EU has a number of potential partners for parts of its engagement in Turkmenistan and Uzbekistan—the Russian Federation, Kazakhstan and Turkey.

The question of security and energy interests in the region needs to be carefully considered by the EU. While the region faces a number of security challenges, the single largest security threat to the region's stability is the violence being perpetrated against the population by the political regimes themselves.

The EU has come a long way in a short time in terms of upgrading its relations with the countries of Central Asia.

A key immediate task is to improve the EU's communication strategy in relation to its policies in Central Asia. This should be aimed at alerting interested parties in Europe, but also at reaching out and informing individuals, groups and networks in Central Asia of the EU and its policies. The fact that the council's special representative for Central Asia, Pierre

Morel, now also holds a similar position in relation to Georgia which is regarded by many as a sign of disinterest in Central Asia.

The EU has now advocated the questions of dialogue and engagement as the principal means of approaching the countries of Uzbekistan and Turkmenistan. If this is to be successful, thought needs to be given to the aim of this dialogue. What are the costs of dialogue with the authoritarian regimes of the region—loss of credibility with opposition groups, the risks of actually supporting oppressive governments? How broad should dialogue be—should opposition figures, such as Islamists, be included?

The EU still has insufficient capacity and institutional memory with regard to its dealings with Uzbekistan and Turkmenistan. This allows the regimes in these countries to outwit the EU on key issues such as the monitoring of human rights.

The Roles of NATO and the OSCE

NATO [North Atlantic Treaty Organization] has a long-standing relationship with Central Asia through its successful Partnership for Peace (PfP) programme that binds all non-NATO members in the Euro-Atlantic area, including Turkmenistan and Uzbekistan. The alliance was established to defend democracy, but nowadays it also plays an important role in promoting democracy in general and democratic defence reform in specific PfP countries that seek closer ties with the alliance. NATO rarely uses sanctions and normally opts to keep lines of communication open with human rights wrong-doers through the PfP. However, it did cancel most of its activities with Uzbekistan after the Andijon events [military shooting of protesters]. Uzbekistan and Turkmenistan—which are excluded from most regional and international fora—are probably the least active PfP countries.

NATO's role in Turkmenistan and Uzbekistan is extremely limited. NATO has a clear interest in working with both countries in order to gain better access to Afghanistan (the ISAF [International Security Assistance Force] mission).

In the field of democratisation and human rights, NATO barely plays a role in these PfP member states; nor does it do so in terms of democratic defence reform.

The OSCE [Organization for Security and Co-operation in Europe] is present in both countries through an OSCE centre in Ashgabat and a project co-ordinator in Uzbekistan, and both states are members of this troubled organisation. Members are divided over the purpose and tasks of the OSCE. A group of eastern members led by Russia wants the OSCE to be further institutionalised and its main focus to be on security. This group wants to cling strongly to consensus decision making on most, if not all, issues. The second group, led by the US, wants OSCE institutions to function relatively independently while focusing on the human dimension of democracy and human rights. A variety of countries and views lie between these two perspectives. Turkmenistan and Uzbekistan clearly belong to the 'Russia group'.

The OSCE is mainly centred on Turkmenistan and Uzbekistan, doing small but focused projects. The attention paid to work on democratisation and human rights is limited due to a lack of funding and resistance from the Turkmen and Uzbek regimes.

Turkmenistan tends to be clear and open with the OSCE when arguing which issues it is interested in and which it is not.

In 2010, Kazakhstan will chair the OSCE; unfortunately, standards of democracy and human rights in the country have not improved over the last year (and some say they have actually deteriorated). Kazakhstan will have to reform many aspects of its structures in order to meet the 'Madrid obligations' it made during the OSCE ministerial conference held in Madrid in November 2008. Nonetheless, the Kazakh OSCE chairmanship can be considered an opportunity to bring

OSCE members together again and it might have some positive impact on Turkmenistan and Uzbekistan, since attention towards the region will increase as a result of this chairmanship.

Spain will be presiding over the EU Council in the first half of 2010, which provides an opportunity for EU/Spanish foreign policy to coordinate with the Kazakh chairmanship of the OSCE.

The Honduras Truth Commission Faces a Daunting Task

Honduras News

Honduras News is an English-language online news source. In the following viewpoint, the author identifies the members of the Honduran truth commission established to investigate human rights abuses that occurred during the June 2009 political upheaval. The author also finds a growing concern over the honesty and openness of the commission.

As you read, consider the following questions:

1. According to Honduran president Porfirio Lobo, what is the ultimate goal of the truth commission?
2. How does the viewpoint say the commission was established?
3. According to Reina Rivera, how were international members of the truth commission chosen?

President Porfirio Lobo has declared that Honduras's truth commission will commence May 4, 2010.

President Lobo empahasized the independence of the commission, whose ultimate goal is to write an "objective and impartial" account of the incidents surrounding the June 28, 2009, political change of power.

Honduras News, "Truth Commission Faces Daunting Task," *Honduras News*, April 19, 2010. Reprinted by permission.

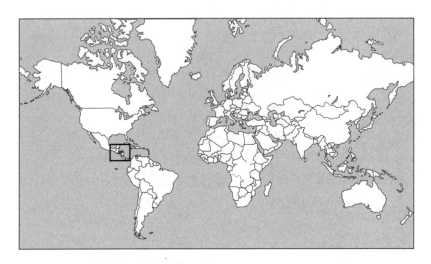

Makeup of the Commission

The commission coordinator is former Guatemalan vice president Eduardo Stein, who served in office from 2004–2008. He will be joined by two other international experts, two national experts and a support team. The Organization of American States (OAS) will be providing technical and administrative assistance.

Mr. Stein stated that it will not be possible for all of the facts uncovered to be made public, because "there will be sensitive information that will be classified, especially confidential testimony provided by certain individuals during the investigation process." He remarked, however, that that information will be declassified and released to the public after a period of ten years.

Eduardo Stein expects that within eight months the findings will be revealed to the Honduran public and stated that "we are going to be extremely scrupulous in our work."

Also serving on the truth commission are internationals Michael Kergin, former assistant deputy minister for the Americas in the Department of Foreign Affairs and International Trade Canada (and Canadian ambassador to the United States from 2000 to 2005); and Maria Amadilia, former minister of justice of Peru.

The two national experts are Hondurans Julieta Castellanos, president of the public National Autonomous University of Honduras (UNAH), and former UNAH president and jurist Jorge Omar Casco. They will be aided by an academic, technical secretary Sergio Membreño.

The Truth and Reconciliation Commission was created to fulfill one of the agreements signed on Oct. 30, 2009, between representatives of President Roberto Micheletti and ousted President Manuel Zelaya. It is also seen as one of the obligations that the Honduran government must fulfill in order to gain recognition from the international community.

Honduran foreign minister, Mario Canahuati, explained that choosing members of the truth commission "was not easy. We studied the curriculum vitae of at least 15 international experts, and on the Honduran side, we tried to seek individuals with a high degree of credibility."

[The Truth and Reconciliation Commission] is also seen as one of the obligations that the Honduran government must fulfill in order to gain recognition from the international community.

The Unión Civica Democrática (Civic Democratic Union) wanted UNAH president Julieta Castellanos removed from the commission, while human rights groups were not happy with the inclusion of Omar Casco, whom they believe represents the most fanatic side of the right-wing politicals.

Skepticism Regarding the Commission

Reina Rivera, a member of the Human Rights Platform coalition, says that the truth commission has met with more skepticism than acceptance among social organizations saying, "We

---

The Alternative Truth Commission

The Human Rights Platform coalition, unconvinced of the impartiality and human rights mandate of the official truth commission, decided to set up and fund its own truth commission with international representatives Adolfo Pérez Esquivel, Rigoberta Menchú, François Houtart, Mirna Antonieta Perla Jiménez, Nora Cortiñas, and Elsie Monje. Its Honduran representatives are Helen Umaña and the Father Fausto Milla. This truth commission is funded by donations from individuals and nongovernmental organizations.

Honduras Culture and Politics,
"Honduras Has Two Truth Commissions," June 22, 2010.

---

believe that the selection of the international members was made more on the basis of their nationalities than their competence and abilities. The representatives from Canada and Peru are not well looked upon in some sectors, which is why some reject the commission, while others view it with reservations."

Ms. Rivera noted that there is already a movement afloat among local and international human rights groups to form an "Alternative Truth Commission." Allegedly Amnesty International is backing it. The purpose of the second commission would be to "monitor the process and the conduct of those who make up the truth commission."

The president of the National Association of Industrialists, Adolfo Facusse, on the other hand, has said that "this truth commission is a demand of the international community and we already know what its findings will be."

Facusse commented that these findings "will be geared to what the world wants to hear, and not to what really happened in Honduras. I don't have very high expectations regarding this question. It won't contribute to reconciliation; on the contrary, it will create greater division."

The Human Rights Platform criticized in a press release that the creation of the truth commission "has not respected the international standards applicable to truth commissions." Pointing out that no consultation process has been opened, nor have the types of violations to be investigated been established.

An Enormous Challenge

In response to these comments, Canahuati stated that "all of this has been contemplated. The commission has freedom and independence. Human rights violations will be considered; we do not want anything to be hidden."

Honduras' first ever human rights commissioner (from 1992 to 2002) is Leo Valladares, who surmises that the doubts stem from "a thirst for justice and truth. It's only natural that there is widespread distrust," he said.

"The commission is facing an enormous challenge, because it must demonstrate its independence and its credibility, and above all, it must prove that it is capable of bringing about a change in the conduct of the Honduran political class," according to Mr. Valladares.

"We shouldn't expect spectacular results from this commission, because it faces heavy resistance," he warned. "But the state has the obligation to investigate."

Periodical and Internet Sources Bibliography

The following articles have been selected to supplement the diverse views presented in this chapter.

Ali el-Bahnasawy	"Emergency Session," *Egypt Today*, June 2010.
Buenos Aires Herald	"Argentines Try Probing Crimes of Franco's Spain," October 12, 2010.
Sebastian Castaneda	"Colombia's Irresponsible Reaction to Human Rights Reports," *Colombia Reports*, March 24, 2010.
Jane Duncan	"Media Freedom Is Your Freedom (or Is It?)," *Pambazuka News* (Africa), September 9, 2010.
Alain Gresh	"Gaza Sinks Slowly," *Le Monde diplomatique* (Paris, France), June 1, 2010.
William Hague	"Human Rights Are Key to Our Foreign Policy," *Telegraph* (UK), August 31, 2010.
Francis Kornegay	"South Sudan: Africa, Bashir, and the ICC," *Pambazuka News* (Africa), September 16, 2010.
Garry Leech	"The U.S. and Colombian Role in the Honduran Crisis," *Colombia Journal*, October 27, 2009.
Peter Mwaura	"Overzealous Officials Can Violate Your Rights in 'Public Interest,'" *Daily Nation* (Kenya), September 10, 2010.
Press Trust of India	"At UN, India Slams Pakistan for Sponsoring Terrorism in J&K," New Delhi Television Limited, September 29, 2010. www.ndtv.com.
L. Muthoni Wanyeki	"Don't Pussyfoot with Bashir, Face Reality," *Pambazuka News* (Africa), September 7, 2010.

**GLOBAL**VIEWPOINTS

CHAPTER 3

Human Rights and Minority Populations

Global Caste-Based Discrimination Should Be Treated as a Human Rights Violation

Nicola McNaughton

Nicola McNaughton is a contributor to New Statesman. *In the following viewpoint, McNaughton describes the condition of the dalits in India, who are referred to as the "untouchables" ranked at the bottom of the Hindu religious hierarchy on the basis of family descent. Discrimination on the basis of caste was outlawed by the Indian Constitution and is not prominent in cities but is still practiced in rural areas, for example, in the continued practice of employment of dalits for manual scavenging, a trade that involves emptying human waste from non-flushing toilets. McNaughton mentions three organizations that have been formed to oppose caste discrimination and to promote the rights of dalits. The Dalit Solidarity Network, a UK-based organization, is trying to raise awareness of the corporate social responsibility of UK-based companies doing business in India and South Asia. The International Dalit Solidarity Network (IDSN) strives to influence international institutions about policies and practices related to caste discrimination. Safai Karmachari Andolan (SKA) is a dalit movement committed to the eradication of manual scavenging in India.*

As you read, consider the following questions:

1. How many of India's twenty-eight states adopted the Employment of Manual Scavengers and Construction of Dry Latrines (Prohibition) Act, according to the viewpoint?
2. What are the Ambedkar Principles endorsed by the Dalit Solidarity Network?
3. In how many of India's twenty-eight states does the Safai Karmachari Andolan (SKA) have an active presence?

Despite the international perception of India, social discrimination based on the outlawed caste system is still intact.

In 2010, the Commonwealth Games will take place in Delhi, India's capital under the slogan 'Humanity, Equality, Destiny'. To many, this may seem appropriate—earlier this year the country underwent its fifteenth general election since independence. 714 million registered to vote, reinforcing India's position as the largest functioning democracy in the world. But for millions of people in India, these concepts are far from reality.

But in small towns and villages where the caste system is still prominent, higher castes refuse to purchase from or associate themselves with dalits [who try to set up their own non-scavenging business]. As a result, these people are forced back into manual scavenging to make enough money to survive.

Social discrimination based on the outlawed caste system is still very much intact. There are approximately 200 million dalits living in India—also referred to as 'scheduled castes' or 'untouchables'. These people are ranked at the bottom of the Hindu religious hierarchy on account of family descent, and as a result, are forced into social deprivation.

The Indian Constitution outlawed discrimination on the basis of caste. Indeed, over the past 60 years, caste barriers have largely broken down in cities, but in rural areas where approximately 70 per cent of India's population lives, they are still prominent. Even the country's prime minister, Manmohan Singh, acknowledges the problem—"after 60 years of constitutional legal protection and support . . . dalits face a unique discrimination in [Indian] society that is fundamentally different from the problems of minority groups in general. The only parallel to the practice of untouchability [is] apartheid."

Sharadah is a dalit who lives in a small village in Gujarat—a resource rich state in western India. At 3 a.m. she begins her daily routine as one of India's 1.3 million manual scavengers. Her job involves going around local houses emptying the human waste from non-flushing toilets. After she has collected the waste using a brush and large drum, she carries the drum on her head, walking 4 kilometers to dispose of the contents. Many manual scavengers like Sharadah have tried to escape the manual scavenging trade, setting up alternative businesses. But in small towns and villages where the caste system is still prominent, higher castes refuse to purchase from or associate themselves with dalits. As a result, these people are forced back into manual scavenging to make enough money to survive.

Manual scavenging is a typical job assigned to dalits in India. In 1993, in response to growing domestic and international pressure from human rights groups, the Indian government passed the Employment of Manual Scavengers and Construction of Dry Latrines (Prohibition) Act. The act prohibits the employment of manual scavengers and the construction of dry toilets not connected to proper drainage channels. Violations of the act can lead to imprisonment for up to one year or a substantial fine of 2,000 Indian rupees. In spite of this, a 2003 government impact assessment of the act found that the law had only been adopted in 16 of India's 28 states, and has not been enforced in any.

The act is a typical example of a 'white elephant' policy, implemented as a short-term measure to shake off interest group pressure. It is clear that without the inclusion of clear provisions for tackling the deeper issue of caste-based discrimination, that it was an impossible law to implement.

A number of interest groups are currently working to influence change from different angles. More focus needs to be brought to groups who are striving for social change through creative methods, challenging the social system through international pressure and through empowerment of the dalits themselves.

The Dalit Solidarity Network [DSN] is a UK-based network of individuals, groups and organisations working with dalit communities in Asia to end global caste-based discrimination. Alongside government lobbying and advocacy initiatives, DSN-UK has undertaken an action study 'Another Apartheid? Caste Discrimination and UK Companies' in response to growing economic investment in India by UK-based companies in recent years. Through case study investigations into eight different UK-based organisations operating in India, DSN-UK has sought to develop an understanding of employment practices by foreign investors in India with regard to the dalit community.

"Our aim [by undertaking this study] was to open up dialogue and work with the corporate sector to inform best practice with regard to caste and caste discrimination" says Meena Varma, director of the Dalit Solidarity Network. "It is not surprising . . . that few companies, especially those moving to South Asia for the first time are aware of caste discrimination. There is a real opportunity for global corporations in India to address caste through their employment, corporate social responsibility (CSR) and—in the case of banks—financing policies."

131

The published report includes a number of key recommendations for private investors, one of which is to encourage adoption of the Ambedkar Principles—a set of guidelines developed in 2004 which suggest numerous ways for international investors to strengthen the dalit workforce in caste-affected countries. The principles recommend that companies provide in-house training programmes about the caste system and emphasise the importance of complying with national legislation on the subject.

Another organisation is taking the issue of caste discrimination to the international level, encouraging discussion and awareness at international institutions including the UN [United Nations] and the EU [European Union]. The International Dalit Solidarity Network (IDSN) is an international network of organisations which strives to link grassroots priorities with international institutions in order to change policies and practices related to caste discrimination worldwide. They have a secretariat in Copenhagen, Denmark.

In November, coordinator of IDSN Rikke Nöhrlind visited Brussels with three dalit representatives from India and Nepal to discuss the extent of caste discrimination in India and South Asia. The occasion was a briefing for members of the Asia-Oceania Working Party (COASI) and Working Party on Human Rights (COHOM)—two EU working groups responsible for Asia-Europe relations and human rights respectively.

The overall purpose of the November visit was to explore how the EU can address caste discrimination in its interaction with caste-affected countries through development cooperation, trade relations and political dialogues. The delegation also urged the EU to take the issue further at the European Council level and to continue its support within the UN framework. A set of UN principles and guidelines has been developed on the basis of existing human rights principles and obligations, proposing measures for governments and other actors to prevent and address caste discrimination. The

India's Caste System Is Firmly Rooted

To be born a Hindu in India is to enter the caste system, one of the world's longest surviving forms of social stratification. Embedded in Indian culture for the past 1,500 years, the caste system follows a basic precept: All men are created unequal. The ranks in Hindu society come from a legend in which the main groupings, or varnas, emerge from a primordial being. From the mouth come the Brahmans—the priests and teachers. From the arms come the Kshatriyas—the rulers and soldiers. From the thighs come the Vaisyas—merchants and traders. From the feet come the Sudras—laborers. Each varna in turn contains hundreds of hereditary castes and subcastes with their own pecking orders.

A fifth group describes the people who are achuta, or untouchable. The primordial being does not claim them. Untouchables are outcasts—people considered too impure, too polluted to rank as worthy beings. Prejudice defines their lives, particularly in the rural areas, where nearly three-quarters of India's people live. Untouchables are shunned, insulted, banned from temples and higher-caste homes, made to eat and drink from separate utensils in public places, and, in extreme but not uncommon cases, are raped, burned, lynched, and gunned down.

The ancient belief system that created the untouchables overpowers modern law. While India's constitution forbids caste discrimination and specifically abolishes untouchability, Hinduism, the religion of 80 percent of India's population, governs daily life with its hierarchies and rigid social codes.

Tom O'Neill, "Untouchable,"
National Geographic Magazine, *June 2003.*

UN High Commissioner for Human Rights, Navi Pillay, recently urged the international community to endorse the guidelines and "eradicate the shameful concept of caste".

Whilst efforts from organisations such as these are invaluable in slowly encouraging change to occur, the most important type of work for dalits such as Sharadah is empowerment from the grassroots upwards. In conjunction with international projects and advocacy efforts, grassroots-level initiatives are vital in challenging the social constructs of society.

Representatives from SKA hold local meetings with manual scavengers throughout India, engaging the workers in discussion on the issue of manual scavenging, exposing its links to the caste system and identifying the inherent problems associated with the occupation.

Safai Karmachari Andolan (SKA) is a dalit movement committed to the eradication of manual scavenging in India. It was initiated in 1986 by a group of human rights activists in the state of Karnataka. Over the past twenty years, the organisation has grown substantially, and now focuses predominantly on organising and mobilising manual scavengers around the issues of dignity and rights.

In order to do this, representatives from SKA hold local meetings with manual scavengers throughout India, engaging the workers in discussion on the issue of manual scavenging, exposing its links to the caste system and identifying the inherent problems associated with the occupation. They aim to raise awareness among the community about their rights under the law, and strive to improve the capacity of these workers to enable them to advocate for their own rights and to challenge their own position in society.

SKA also seeks to identify manual scavengers willing to work for their community, and trains them to take on work as full-time SKA activists. These trainings centre on building perspectives on the links between the caste system and manual scavenging, human rights, developing skills of mobilisation, strategising interventions, leadership and articulation skills, as well as networking and alliance building at different levels.

Through conducting activities like these and building networks with like-minded individuals, SKA has rolled out and expanded their work across India—from its inception as a small group of social activists, SKA now has an active presence in 16 states across India. Movements like this show glimmers of hope for the future of the dalit population.

'Humanity', 'Equality' and 'Destiny' are a far cry from the existing state of Indian society, and this is unlikely to change before the Commonwealth Games commence next year. The caste system is a deeply entrenched issue in Indian society. However, the hosting of the games is an ideal opportunity to put India in the spotlight, encouraging more initiatives like SKA and bringing awareness to advocacy efforts like those undertaken by DSN-UK and IDSN.

China Continues to Tyrannize the Uyghur Minority

Amy Reger

Amy Reger is the principal researcher for the Uyghur American Association's Uyghur Human Rights Project. In the following viewpoint, she contends that the international community should learn more about the Uyghur people and the discrimination they endure at the hands of Chinese authorities. Reger asserts that the Chinese government justifies its repression of the Uyghurs by citing national security concerns.

As you read, consider the following questions:

1. How many border police were killed in August 2008 in Kashgar, East Turkestan, allegedly by two young Uyghur men?
2. What kind of human rights abuses do more than ten million Uyghurs of East Turkestan face?
3. Why was Nurmuhemmet Yasin imprisoned, according to Reger?

In the tiny offices of the Uyghur American Association/ Uyghur Human Rights Project, our phones have rung off the hook since Monday morning [August 2008]. Journalists from four continents have called to hear our comments regarding Monday's attack in Kashgar, East Turkestan, in which

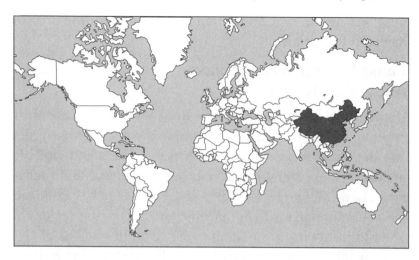

16 border police were killed. Chinese government authorities are reporting that the attack was carried out by two young Uyghur men, a fruit vendor and a taxi driver. Acts of this nature threaten to undermine the progress we have made in peaceful Uyghur human rights advocacy in a single blow. They also threaten to instantly reduce the Uyghur people and their rich cultural tapestry into a one-dimensional image of violence in the minds of millions.

While we welcome all media inquiries, it is unfortunate that an appalling, violent act such as this has been the impetus for an unprecedented level of interest in Uyghurs and in our organization, which is dedicated to peacefully promoting human rights and democracy for the Uyghur people. It is a tragedy that for most people around the world hearing news of the attack, this is the first time they will have ever heard of the Uyghur people—and now, in their minds, the word "Uyghur" will be associated with violence and the word "terrorism" that is splashed across the headlines of the world's newspapers. Unsubstantiated links to al Qaeda proffered by China's official media have been widely republished in many Western news reports—the suggested linkage is too newsworthy to ignore, yet at the same time impossible for deadline-pressed media to independently check out.

China Spreads Propaganda About the Uyghurs

Unfortunately for Uyghurs, they live in a world where their belief in Islam, despite their strongly pro-Western attitudes and the traditionally moderate practice of their faith, unfairly brands them as a group that is prone to violence and fundamentalism. Moreover, the Chinese government has exploited the demonization of Islam and the "global war on terror" in order to justify its heavy-handed repression of millions of Uyghurs. China's propaganda apparatus has become increasingly sophisticated at projecting an image on the world stage of a major, well-organized Uyghur terrorist threat, which helps to crowd out discussion of the decades-long history of human rights abuses visited upon the Uyghurs.

The more than ten million Uyghurs of East Turkestan face human rights abuses nearly identical to those faced by Tibetans: arbitrary detention and imprisonment, religious repression, economic and educational discrimination, and the steady eradication of their language and culture from public life and institutions. While many people around the world have some knowledge of the suffering of the Tibetan people (thanks to decades of courageous advocacy on the part of Tibetans and their supporters), and a sympathetic view of Buddhism, relatively few have heard of the Uyghurs and their plight, and their religion makes it easy for people to accept Chinese government assertions about Muslim "extremism" among Uyghurs. In addition, the Chinese government frequently applies the "terrorist" label to Uyghurs where it would use the term "separatist" to describe Tibetans or other groups.

The World Must Learn the Truth

The Uyghur American Association's small staff faces a daunting challenge—how to compete with a relentless Chinese government propaganda machine, and attempt to inform the world about human rights abuses committed against a people they've probably never heard of except in relation to a violent act. We must also attempt to ensure that no one misinterprets our human rights advocacy as an attempt to downplay or justify a terrible act of aggression. We face an uphill battle against facile sensationalism, exploited by the Chinese government; we are also competing against a sea of Olympics [held in China in 2008] puff pieces and "colour stories" produced by multimillion-dollar television news outlets. Relatively few news outlets dare to venture out of comfortable territory to produce nuanced pieces on Uyghurs or similarly nontraditional subjects.

China's propaganda apparatus . . . helps to crowd out discussion of the decades-long history of human rights abuses visited upon the Uyghurs.

However, facing a much graver set of circumstances are the Uyghur people in East Turkestan themselves, and particularly Uyghurs in Kashgar, who are now being subjected to even greater intimidation and persecution than ever before. We have reliable reports of Uyghurs being summarily rounded up in one area of Kashgar in the past week; police going door to door in Uyghur neighborhoods and checking everyone's identity papers; the closure of at least one mosque in the city; and the stepped-up blockage of Internet access.

Poor Treatment of the Uyghur People

In recent months in East Turkestan, Uyghurs' passports have been almost universally confiscated by authorities; large numbers of Uyghurs have been evicted from major cities in East Turkestan, including those who had legal rights to stay in those cities; and at least one mosque was destroyed, appar-

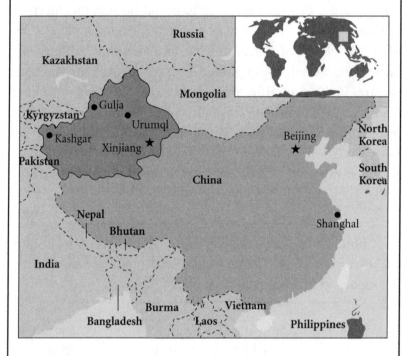

The Xinjiang Province, China's Largest Province and Home of the Uyghur People

47% of Xinjiang is Uyghur; 41% is Han, the majority ethnic group in China.

TAKEN FROM: "China–Silenced," *Frontline World*, January 2005.

ently due to parishioners' refusal to post Olympics slogans on its walls. In addition, Uyghurs in East Turkistan have been told to avoid contact with foreigners, especially foreign journalists, and Uyghur imams [religious leaders] have been ordered to undergo "political education" regarding the Olympics.

Many Uyghurs who had been living in Beijing have been forced to leave the city, and official directives have been issued to hotels and guesthouses throughout Beijing not to permit Uyghurs to stay there.

On July 9 [2008], five young Uyghurs were shot to death without warning by police in the regional capital of Ürümchi, in a raid on an alleged "holy war training group". On the same day, following a mass sentencing rally in Kashgar, two Uyghurs were executed and 15 others were handed sentences ranging from 10 years in prison to death on unsubstantiated terror-related charges. Schoolchildren were among the 10,000 Uyghurs forced to attend the rally.

We urge readers to ... educate yourself about the harsh, government-sponsored suppression that is threatening to eradicate Uyghurs' culture and way of life.

Demonizing the Uyghur People

Since 2001, using "terrorism" as justification, the Chinese government has undertaken a renewed, systematic, and sustained crackdown on all forms of Uyghur dissent. Those targeted in this crackdown include two sons of Uyghur freedom movement leader Rebiya Kadeer, Alim and Ablikim Abdureyim, serving lengthy prison sentences because of their mother's Uyghur human rights advocacy (Ms. Kadeer is president of the Uyghur American Association); Nurmuhemmet Yasin, a young intellectual imprisoned for writing a story about a pigeon that authorities deemed subversive; and schoolteacher Abdulghani Memetemin, imprisoned for providing documentation of human rights abuses to an overseas group.

While the Chinese government promotes an image of itself as a nation unified in ethnic brotherhood, in the manner of the Olympics slogan "One World, One Dream," it is simultaneously demonizing the Uyghur people as a whole. It has every right to condemn a violent attack on its soil, and to secure itself against the threat of violence and terrorism throughout the PRC [People's Republic of China]. But the killings in Kashgar should not be used as an excuse to continue and even intensify egregious human rights abuses in East Turkestan.

141

They should also not be used as a vehicle to exacerbate tensions between Han Chinese and Uyghurs.

The international community should also refrain from judging the Uyghur people as a whole on the actions of a tiny minority. We urge readers to learn more about the Uyghur people and their rich Turkic heritage and culture; to visit East Turkestan if you are traveling to China to attend the Olympics; and to educate yourself about the harsh, government-sponsored suppression that is threatening to eradicate Uyghurs' culture and way of life.

Estonia Is Discriminating Against Ethnic Russians

Kai Joost

Kai Joost is a reporter for Baltic Reports, a website devoted to news concerning the Baltic states. In the following viewpoint, Joost reports that Estonia often overlooks the widespread discrimination against ethnic Russians living in the region. Part of the friction between Estonians and ethnic Russians is the heated debate over how Russians came to live in the region years ago.

As you read, consider the following questions:

1. According to Marju Lauristin, why doesn't Estonia deal with issues of discrimination adequately?
2. When did Estonia's first law handling discrimination issues come into effect?
3. During what period was Estonia a Soviet republic?

A fter 20 years of Estonian independence, ethnic Russians and other minorities continue to face discrimination according to the United Nations [UN] and European Union [EU].

A UN Human Rights Council report from 2007 said little concrete action was being taken on issues such as the statelessness of ethnic Russians and the language policy.

The depth of the problem was also addressed at the European Union's Equality Summit in Stockholm [the capital of

Kai Joost, "Ethnic Russians Have It Tough in Estonia," Baltic Reports, February 2, 2010. Reprinted by permission.

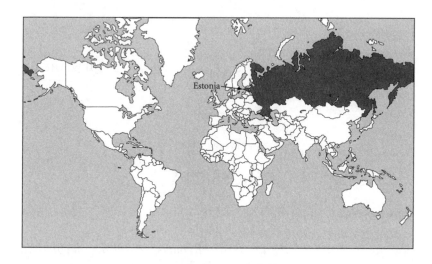

Sweden] in November [2009] where many top EU and non-governmental organization officials said the Baltic states are failing to uphold human rights and equal treatment of minorities.

Discrimination Is Ignored in Estonia

Marju Lauristin, a professor at the University of Tartu, is concerned that discrimination is not dealt with enough in Estonia, and even using the word discrimination is taboo.

"In most of European countries there is a minister, and many different programs dealing with this issue," Lauristin told Baltic Reports. "Estonia is not yet a mature democratic society, and it lacks people who would dare to handle this issue."

Lauristin considered the word discrimination as another problem as many people don't even know what that word means.

"Discrimination means when the laws don't apply to all people equally," told Lauristin.

The first law handling discrimination issues, the Equal Treatment Act, came into force only in Jan. 1, 2009.

Cases of Discrimination Make Headlines

Meanwhile cases of discrimination continue to make headlines. In Sept. 2009 Eiki Strauss, an orthopedic surgeon in Kohtla-Järve, a small town in northeastern Estonia, threw a 14-year-old boy's passport into the trash can because the boy did not speak Estonian. Strauss argued in the explanatory letter that because the boy did not speak the state language, he therefore should not hold Estonian citizenship. The incident ... happened in a region of Estonia where Russian is widely spoken.

Maksim, [age] 28 of Tallinn, is an ethnic Russian information technology worker and asked that his last name not be used. He told Baltic Reports that it is harder to get a job for him than ethnic Estonians he knows, and getting a national passport is a difficult process.

"I don't have any other homeland besides Estonia, Russia is not my home," Maksim said. He still carries an alien passport.

Discrimination is not limited to ethnic Russians, of course. Nuno Antas, [age] 28 from Portugal, lived in the small town of Võru in southern Estonia in 2007, working as a volunteer at a day care center for disabled people.

Nuno once received a threatening letter that read: "We know what you've been doing here! Leave us Estonians alone and go away from our land! You are not welcome here, and we're following you." Another was addressed to him on the Rate.ee social networking website, saying, "You do not belong in Võru, you f------ n-----. You must die!"

The Source Lies in History

Researchers point to Estonia's history of foreign subjugation as a primary source of antipathy toward other ethnicities.

Estonia has been a hot spot for foreign invaders throughout history, ruled by Sweden, Denmark, Germany and Russia.

Most recently, from 1945 until 1991 the country was a Soviet republic. More than 80,000 people were deported to Siberia for various reasons and education was carried out in Russian.

The Nature of Russification Is Disputed

A legacy of the Soviet era is the large Russian ethnic minority, and why they ended up in Estonia is considered a source of the friction.

Some researchers, such as Kristina Kallas, an analyst and board member of the Institute of Baltic Studies, discount the more widely known theory on [former dictator Joseph] Stalin's Russification policies that brought the ethnic Russians to Estonia and instead point to economic factors.

"The members of the Communist Party and soldiers were less than 5 percent of the migrants, most of the migrants were usual blue collars, miners and factory workers with 9th grade education," Kallas told Baltic Reports. "I am not pushing over the claim that Stalin had other intentions as well besides industrialization, such as Russification, but the Russian workers had no instructions for that."

> *A legacy of the Soviet era is the large Russian ethnic minority, and why they ended up in Estonia is considered a source of the friction.*

Kallas explained that the Russian laborer, just like an Estonian, was also the victim of Soviet policies and was sent to work in the Baltic country without their consent.

"Stalin wanted to industrialize and the heavy immigration came with it," Kallas said.

Another View of the Problem

This historical narrative is disputed. Tõnu Tannberg, a history professor at the University of Tartu, said that he does not agree with Kallas's statements.

"Of course the process was affected by economic and demographic reasons," Tannberg told Baltic Reports. "However, it would be naive to consider that the change of population's ethnic composition wouldn't have been pleasing for Moscow."

Vahur Made, historian and deputy director of the Estonian School of Diplomacy, called Kallas's arguments cynical.

"From a historian's point of view this text is so cynical that it is even hard to comment on it in a reasonable way," Made told Baltic Reports.

Made insisted that Stalin's decisions cannot be certified by population statistics and would need an access to Russian archives which Estonian researchers practically do not have.

"Russia has widely used its colonizing politics and is using the technique in the present, routing the Russians to non-Russian regions," told Made.

Sudan Violates the Human Rights of Its Citizens

Lotte Leicht

*Lotte Leicht was Human Rights Watch's European Union direc-
tor at the time of writing. In the following viewpoint, Leicht argues that the international pressure of sanctions is needed to put
an end to the scorched-earth campaign of killings, rape, destruction, and displacement by the Sudanese government forces and
their allied Janjaweed militias. The International Criminal Court
has issued warrants for some of the perpetrators, but these warrants have been ignored by the Sudanese. Some of the perpetrators even hold official government posts; therefore, they have a
feeling of impunity from repercussions. Leicht calls upon the
British prime minister to impose the sanctions that he promised
if progress failed or human rights violations continued.*

As you read, consider the following questions:

1. According to Leicht, how many troops did the UN approve for deployment in Sudan and how effectively were
   they deployed?
2. Who is Ahmed Haroun, and what does Leicht say about
   his political career?
3. What sanctions does Leicht want the EU to impose on
   Sudan?

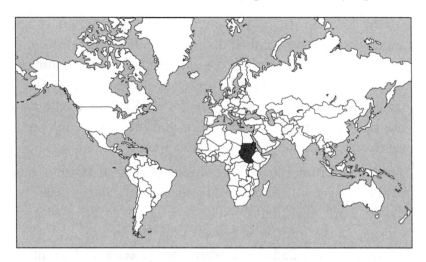

Shortly after taking office, UK [United Kingdom] Prime Minister Gordon Brown stood before the United Nations General Assembly and declared the situation in Darfur to be the "greatest humanitarian disaster" facing the world today. He sent a message to Darfur that "it is time for change".

Brown pledged to place sanctions on the Sudanese government if the killings of civilians in Darfur did not stop. Nine months later, people are still dying and suffering—apparently, Khartoum [the capital of Sudan] did not get the message. It is time to send it with a new messenger—sanctions.

Many in Europe have never heard of Ahmed Haroun, but for the villagers of Bindisi, Kodoom, Arawala and Mukjar, he is their worst nightmare.

While Brown and French President Nicolas Sarkozy should be applauded for their efforts last year [2007] which resulted in the adoption of a United Nations resolution approving the deployment of a 26,000 strong peacekeeping force to Sudan, President [Omar al-]Bashir has managed to obstruct and delay this deployment.

The UK and its EU [European Union] partners have responded to Bashir's continued stonewalling with only kid gloves and toothless threats. Despite pledges to the contrary, the EU has still not imposed sanctions to encourage Bashir's compliance. Without firmer pressure on Khartoum, the victims of Darfur will never see justice, and their persecutors will feel free to redouble their murderous ways.

Many in Europe have never heard of Ahmed Haroun, but for the villagers of Bindisi, Kodoom, Arawala and Mukjar, he is their worst nightmare. Four years ago, Haroun was State Minister of the Interior responsible for Darfur's security during the time that Sudanese government forces and their allied Janjaweed militias carried out a brutal scorched-earth campaign of killings, rape, destruction and displacement.

Haroun and those under his watch are alleged to have murdered hundreds, raped women and young girls, destroyed property, and forcibly removed thousands from their homes. Some of the crimes were carried out by a militia leader named Ali Mohammed Ali, also known as "Ali Kosheib," who received orders from Haroun.

Since then, the International Criminal Court [ICC] has charged Ahmed Haroun and "Ali Kosheib" with 51 counts of crimes against humanity and war crimes, including murder, rape, persecution and forcible transfer of population.

Despite international arrest warrants issued almost one year ago, Haroun and Kosheib remain free men. Indeed, far from having arrested Haroun, the Sudanese government promoted him; he is currently Sudan's sitting Minister of State for Humanitarian Affairs. Then, to add insult to injury, Khartoum appointed Haroun co-chair of a committee that monitors security in Sudan and is authorized to hear complaints of victims of abuses, including those in Darfur. By virtue of his position, Haroun is also the intermediary between the government and the UN forces designated to protect civilians. The

"Wanted: Al-Bashir of Sudan for crimes against humanity," cartoon by Wilfred Hildonen, CartoonStock.com. Copyright © Wilfred Hildonen. Reproduction rights available from www.CartoonStock.com.

second ICC suspect, "Ali Kosheib," was imprisoned at the time the arrest warrants were issued, but the Sudanese government has since released him.

Developments in Darfur over the past year have been bleak. Peace talks have stalled—again; ceasefires are violated on almost a daily basis; government-backed forces have shot at clearly marked UN convoys and have bombed civilians; and armed men in uniform have looted villages and raped women. The rate of atrocities committed and documented in the last three months alone is now reminiscent of the beginning of the scorched-earth campaign in 2003-2004. Such is the "progress" that has been made in Darfur while the world and the EU sat back and adopted a "wait and see approach".

One of the factors arguably contributing to this downward spiral is that the Sudanese government has not seen any real consequence for its continued repression in Darfur and its continued obstruction of international efforts to curb that repression. Khartoum has simply ignored UN resolutions and international arrest warrants with no repercussions.

Khartoum's intransigence may be expected, but the lack of a firm EU response is deeply disappointing. The UK and the EU tout international justice as a priority, but it has left the ICC prosecutor empty-handed as he seeks pressure on Khartoum to surrender indicted suspects for trial. Until significant costs are imposed on it, Khartoum has no incentive to stop its current campaign of atrocities or to cooperate with the ICC.

When a government grants official posts to people accused of war crimes, it is long past time to transcend empty threats and apply meaningful pressure.

Indeed, over the past year, Khartoum's lack of cooperation has evolved into overt defiance, if not mockery. In January, for example, President Bashir created a special presidential advisory position for a notorious Janjaweed leader who is subject to UN sanctions. With alleged war criminals serving in political posts, Khartoum has clearly sent the world a message: It may have to allow a peacekeeping force in Darfur, but it does not have to give the victims any justice.

Three years ago, the UK was instrumental in securing the historic referral of the Darfur crimes to the ICC. At the time of the referral, the UN Security Council took the view that justice was an essential component of any effort to end the violence in Darfur. But since then, British and EU leaders have, by and large, turned their backs on the principle of justice.

When a government grants official posts to people accused of war crimes, it is long past time to transcend empty threats and apply meaningful pressure. Otherwise, the Sudanese government will only be reconfirmed in its view that it can continue to commit atrocities in Darfur with impunity.

In an EU declaration issued 31 March, the EU threatened punitive measures against those responsible for Sudan's failure to cooperate with the ICC, including the failure to arrest and surrender those subject to international arrest warrants to the court. It is up to the EU to ensure that this declaration will not be just the latest example in a long history of empty threats that the rulers in Khartoum have become so accustomed to ignoring with impunity.

In keeping with Brown's commitment to redouble efforts to impose further sanctions if any party blocked progress or the killings continued in Darfur, the UK should assume the lead in demanding that EU leaders take the next step when they meet in June and adopt targeted individual sanctions against those officials who are responsible not only for Sudan's serious human rights violations but also for its non-cooperation with the ICC. Such sanctions should include visa bans and travel restrictions, the freezing of assets, and the blocking of access to European banking systems.

Justice isn't simply a moral luxury. The EU made a pledge to the victims of Darfur; it is high time that the EU delivered—that it moved from empty threats to action.

Iranian Persecution of the Bahá'í Is an Injustice and Rejection of True Iranian Identity

Payam Akhavan

Payam Akhavan is a professor of international law at McGill University in Montreal. In the following viewpoint, he contends that the brutal and systematic repression of the Bahá'í community in Iran is a crime against humanity and the identity of the Iranian people. Akhavan argues that this harsh treatment is a reflection of a national government that propagates violence and exclusion and does not respect the intrinsic value of all people.

As you read, consider the following questions:

1. How does Akhavan identify democracy and human rights for the Iranian people?
2. What does the author see as the consequences of disregarding our shared humanity?
3. How can the Bahá'í people be persecuted under the Iranian constitution?

What does it mean to be Iranian? What does it mean to be a human being? These are the questions confronting the Iranian people at this crucial juncture in their long his-

Payam Akhavan, "The Baha'i Community, Human Rights, and the Construction of a New Iranian Identity," *Iran Press Watch*, February 27, 2010. Reprinted by permission.

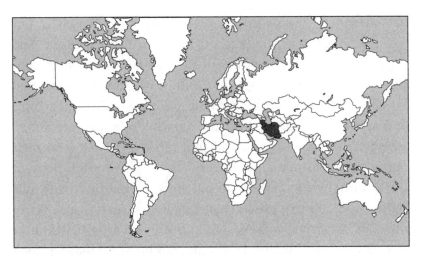

tory. In the incredible and unforgettable scenes that have unfolded in the streets of Tehran [Iran's capital], and Isfahan, and Shiraz, and Tabriz, and Mashhad, and Ahvaz, and every other city and town in Iran, we are witnessing a struggle far greater than a mere political contest between different presidential candidates. We are witnessing a struggle for the soul of the nation; a struggle to build a new identity for the Iranian people. The encounter between the protestors and their tormentors is an encounter between the dark past and the bright future. It is an encounter between violence and nonviolence, between the courage of those that are willing to sacrifice their lives for justice, and the cowardice of those that savagely beat and murder the defenseless. It is an encounter between the best and worst potentials inherent in humankind.

Human Rights and Iranian Identity

The millions marching in the streets, youth and women, student and labour movements, intellectuals and artists, webloggers and journalists, a social movement of unprecedented unity and resolve, have demonstrated that without legitimacy there can be no lasting power. They have demonstrated vividly the deeper meaning of the words democracy, human rights, and the rule of law; words that we throw about loosely in our world without always appreciating the price that must be paid for its attainment. The power of their demands lies in its simplicity. The Iranian people are asking whether the God that we all worship and all that we hold sacred, whether the dreams and aspirations that we have for our children, they are asking whether these do not demand that those in power treat their citizens with justice and equality. They ask why the hope of our youth in the future should be extinguished, why our mothers and sisters should be treated with such disrespect in our laws, why our workers should live in such poverty amidst our national wealth, and why a utopian ideology that has long promised both freedom and prosperity has achieved neither.

For the people of Iran, democracy and human rights are not intellectual abstractions. Freedom and tolerance are not about idle theological disputes. For them, these are existential needs in the face of a daily onslaught of violence, deception, corruption, and hatred. For them, these demands go to the very meaning of what it means to be Iranian and what it means to be a human being. What they seek simply is an Iranian nation where every citizen enjoys fundamental human rights.

We are witnessing a struggle for the soul of the nation; a struggle to build a new identity for the Iranian people.

Justice, equality, solidarity, a culture where religion gives people spiritual fulfillment rather than serving as a pretext for abuse of power, in struggling for this vision of what it means to be Iranian, the countless youth that have stood firm in the face of savage beatings, murders, and torture speak to a deeper yearning within us all. Through their sacrifices they bring to life the words of the United Nations Universal Declaration of Human Rights that: "All human beings are born free and equal in dignity and rights. They are endowed with reason and conscience and should act towards one another in a spirit of brotherhood."

We Must Recognize the Value of All Human Beings

After thousands of years of historical evolution, through countless wars and revolutions and ideologies, humankind has arrived at the realization that the foundation of civilization and progress is recognition of the inherent dignity of all human beings. That dignity is not premised on whether we belong to an approved religion or race or political ideology or social class. It is part of what it means to be and to treat others as human beings. On the bloodstained pages of contemporary history, from Nazi Germany and Cambodia to Yugoslavia and Rwanda, from Afghanistan and Iraq to Uganda and the Sudan, we witness the devastating consequences of disregarding our shared humanity. The case is no different for the thousands of our fellow Iranians, be they religious or secular, Muslim or Bahá'í, Azeri, Kurdish or Baluchi, Republican or Socialist, man or woman, whose rights have been trampled upon merely because of who they are and what they believe. In the name of Islam, in the name of the divine, those that have arrogated to themselves the right to speak on behalf of God, have murdered and tortured countless sons and daughters of this long-suffering nation. They have corrupted the spiritual longing of its people with the profane lust of wealth and power. The poor in whose name they spoke have become ever more wretched amidst the unprecedented oil wealth of the country. And the end to injustice they promised has brought stoning and hanging of "infidels" and "the corrupt on earth" and "the enemies of God", defined as anybody who dares to challenge the absolute power of self-proclaimed leaders. Women are forcibly veiled to protect men against their own lust and treated as inferior to men that dominate and

---

Bahá'ís Believe

- All humanity is one family.

- Women and men are equal.

- All prejudice—racial, religious, national, or economic—
  is destructive and must be overcome.

- We must investigate truth for ourselves, without
  preconceptions.

- Science and religion are in harmony.

- Our economic problems are linked to spiritual
  problems.

- The family and its unity are very important.

- There is one God.

- All major religions come from God.

- World peace is the crying need of our time.

Bahá'í Faith,
"Bahá'ís Believe," 2010. www.bahai.org.

---

mistreat them with impunity. And those whose religion is not
approved by the State cannot enjoy full rights as citizens. This
is the tragedy and despair that has brought the disillusioned
millions to our streets.

Violating Human Rights Is an Attack on Humanity

The denial of human rights is not only the problem of its direct victims. It is an assault on our common humanness. Nowhere is this more apparent than laws and policies that make

a particular status or belief a crime. In this light, what makes the persecution of Bahá'ís important is not just the Bahá'ís themselves. When the constitution and leaders of the Islamic Republic proclaim that citizens of Iran can be denied the right to education and lawful marriage, dispossessed of their sacred sites, cemeteries, personal property and livelihood, arrested, tortured, and murdered, and subject to slander and hate propaganda, merely because of their religion, this is a crime not just against the Bahá'ís, but also a crime against the Iranian people, and a crime against humanity. Evidently, the historical animosity towards the Bahá'ís and their violent persecution by the Islamic Republic has served a useful function of creating an imaginary enemy against which the masses can be rallied in furtherance of the political ambitions of their leaders' pretension of divine authority. But the injustice has been not only against the Bahá'ís. It has also been an injustice against all Iranian citizens that long for a nation identified with justice and human rights rather than a culture of hatred, self-deception and violence.

To say that there is only one way to be Iranian, whether through the prism of religious, ethnic, or ideological absolutism that leaves no room for diversity, may be reassuring in a world of uncertainty. But it is an abdication of our responsibility to build a future based on human dignity, of shaping our destiny through enlightenment rather than the deceptive comfort of denial and ignorance. Our identity is not an ancient statue in the ruins of Persepolis [an ancient city] waiting to be discovered. Our identity is not to be found in blind imitation of outward pretensions of religious piety. Our identity is a reflection of the moral choices that we make in today's world and our willingness to embrace both our self and the other in a common home. Our identity is a social construction, our nation an imagined community, a shared cultural space in which the lives of our people are intertwined in a mutual search for meaning, prosperity, and progress. Our identity is not fixed in time or place. It is fluid, complex, and constantly evolving. But we have a fundamental choice. And that choice is whether we define ourselves through hatred or humanity.

The historical animosity towards the Bahá'ís and their violent persecution by the Islamic Republic has served a useful function of creating an imaginary enemy against which the masses can be rallied.

Discrimination of Bahá'ís Is Not Part of Iranian Identity

The persecution of Bahá'ís in Iran is not an immutable reality; it is not an irreversible part of Iran's future. It is merely the reflection of the identity that some have tried to impose on the Iranian people. It is the reflection of blind obedience to leaders that elevate hatred to patriotism and transform victims into aggressors. The discrimination against Bahá'ís, the denial of their human rights, the hate propaganda against them, these are merely a particularly notorious manifestation of a culture of exclusion and violence that has afflicted all Iranians that dare to strive for a united nation in which the equal rights of all Iranians are respected. National unity does not mean national homogeneity.

Throughout its history, Iran has been most glorious and most powerful when it has embraced the diversity of its people. The construction of imaginary enemies as an instrument of power, the instigation of hatred and violence against those that dare to be different, this is an affliction on all Iranians, because they stand to lose a future in which their children will live in equality, dignity, and prosperity. By investing so much energy into hate propaganda to blame the Bahá'ís for all the evils of the world, Iran's leaders are only confirming the bankruptcy of their own ideas. They are confirming yet again the irrelevance of a backward ideology that only serves the interests of those in power. Will convincing people that all Bahá'ís are Israeli spies and American agents help explain why Iran's oil wealth has been squandered while people sink into ever greater poverty and misery? Will it explain why our brightest minds are leaving Iran at an accelerating pace? Will it explain why our extraordinary women are treated with such contempt and violence when they merely ask for respect and equality?

Israel Must Safeguard the Rights of All People Within Its Borders

Michael Schwartz

Michael Schwartz is the development director of Rabbis for Human Rights (RHR) and the founder and former director of the Human Rights Yeshiva program at Hebrew University. In the following viewpoint, he maintains that Israel has a unique responsibility to safeguard universal human rights because of the Jewish experience of the Holocaust. Schwartz argues that by exhibiting an unwavering commitment to human rights and peace, the Jewish People and the state of Israel can guarantee a physical and spiritual strength.

As you read, consider the following questions:

1. What does Israel's Declaration of Independence say about human rights?
2. What is the "614th commandment," according to the viewpoint?
3. What does the author say could be a 615th commandment?

Holocaust Remembrance Day memorializes the victims of the Nazis. Observance of this day, though, is also meant to inspire a response from us about how to ensure that such horrible atrocities never occur in our world again.

Michael Schwartz, "The 615th Commandment," *Jerusalem Post*, April 13, 2010. Reprinted by permission of the author.

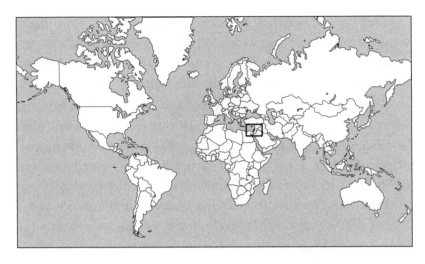

Noted philosopher and theologian, Rabbi Emil Fackenheim, taught that the Holocaust defies any attempt to locate meaning in it. Indeed, it would be scandalously disrespectful to the victims to "justify" their murder by extrapolating some higher meaning from the Shoah's happening, a blasphemy to find some purpose or reason to the presence of such radical evil in God's world and in the capability of human beings—created in God's own image—both to enact such evil and to be victimized by it. And yet, Fackenheim noted, a particularly Jewish response to the Shoah is nevertheless imperative. A universal response of all humanity to the Holocaust is no less obligatory.

It is interesting to note how two very different sets of "responses" to the Shoah are heard frequently among Jews here in Israel and around the world. These two different responses reflect a shared sense of urgent necessity in responding *here today* because of what happened *there then*. At the same time, they demonstrate almost opposite worldviews and understandings of Israel's purpose, and lead toward totally inverse political perspectives and often contradictory activist involvements.

One response is that, essentially, Israel must do anything it wants or needs to do in order to defend itself from hateful enemies set on perpetrating a second holocaust by destroying both the Jewish State and the Jewish People along with it.

The other is that precisely because of our experience as Jews in the Holocaust and through our history littered with injustice and tragedy, we ourselves must make sure that Israel of all places is a nation that stringently safeguards human rights even in the most difficult of circumstances and establishes, in the words of Israel's Declaration of Independence, a nation that "foster[s] the development of the country for the benefit of all its inhabitants; [a nation] based on freedom, justice and peace as envisaged by the prophets of Israel." Indeed, both the physical and spiritual security of the Jewish People and the State of Israel is best guaranteed by the strength of universal human rights law enforced by the collective nations of the world and by Israel's own democracy, its legal system based on the rule of just law, its commitment to human rights, and—ultimately—to the achievement of peace.

Both these responses recognize the absolute importance of protecting the Jewish People and preventing a second Holocaust. In fact, it was the same Rabbi Fackenheim who argued that from the experience of the Holocaust was heard a "614th commandment" in addition to the 613 traditionally found in the Torah: We are commanded not to give Hitler posthumous victories, neither by perishing as a People, by forgetting what was done to us, by denying or despairing of God, nor by ceasing to work towards making the earth a place of holiness, the Kingdom of God. Our failure to observe this new 614th commandment would transform the world into a meaningless place in which God is dead or irrelevant and everything is permitted.

Are these two types of responses to the Holocaust commonly heard amongst Jews today compatible with one another? Does one response or the other better answer the requirements of the 614th commandment? Must some "middle ground" be found, or must we choose one response or the other? How do we respond on this Holocaust Remembrance Day to the real threats that face us even as we wield considerable power and immense responsibility both to protect ourselves and to deal justly, righteously, and honestly with our neighbors, the Palestinians? When Israel strengthens international universal human rights institutions, are its own defenses thereby strengthened?

Fortifying the abilities of Israel and the world community together to defend universal human rights is the best defense of the Jewish People and all other peoples.

Perhaps we can now sense a 615th commandment, born of the 614th and the totality of the 613 before it: We must work to uphold the Torah of universal human rights.

Although the idea of universal human rights has precedents before the Holocaust, it is only after the Shoah—because of the Shoah—that humanity's collective feeling and understanding crystallized around the need for a system of international human rights law and protections. The Preamble to the UDHR clearly notes that the world's attempt to legislate for human rights values is the needed response of humanity to the Holocaust's "barbarous acts which have outraged the conscience of mankind." Indeed, René Cassin—the French Jewish social democrat who played a leading role in drafting the Universal Declaration of Human Rights (UDHR)—observed during the UN General Assembly's debate on accepting the draft of the UDHR, that "something new has entered the world . . . the first document about moral value adopted by an assembly of the human community."

On this Holocaust Remembrance Day, as we memorialize the myriad victims and recall their unimaginable suffering and degradation, Rabbis for Human Rights invites the worldwide Jewish community to consider its response to this "epoch-making event" in our recent history. The formulation of the Universal Declaration of Human Rights, and the international human rights conventions and laws based upon it, is the whole of humanity's best effort to ensure no Holocaust can ever happen again.

A particularly Jewish response to the Holocaust can and must be a turn away from the never-ending fear that our enemies will continue to try to destroy us and instead to turn towards the hope—a wary hope, but hope nonetheless—that fortifying the abilities of Israel and the world community together to defend universal human rights is the best defense of the Jewish People and all other peoples against the kinds of evil whose victims we memorialize today.

Sri Lanka Tries to Escape Accountability for War Crimes Against the Tamil People

Satheesan Kumaaran

Satheesan Kumaaran is a reporter for the Sri Lanka Guardian. *In the following viewpoint, Kumaaran finds that the Sri Lankan government continues to deny its numerous war crimes against the Tamil people. Thus, Kumaaran urges the international community to investigate Sri Lanka and its actions.*

As you read, consider the following questions:

1. What does Kumaaran say is happening when the Tamils try to return to their villages in the Vanni region?
2. How many Tamils were put in concentration camps in Vavuniya, according to the viewpoint?
3. What did video evidence show occurred in 2009 between Tamils and uniformed Sri Lankan soldiers?

After the United People's Freedom Alliance (UPFA) government won the parliamentary election in April this year [2010], Sri Lanka appointed a law professor, G.L. Peiris, as the foreign minister who, for the first time, makes his week-long official visit to the U.S. starting May 23. He met UN [United Nations] secretary-general, Ban Ki-Moon, on May 24th at the

Satheesan Kumaaran, "Sri Lanka Lectures to the World on the Levity of Its War Crimes and Its Serious Breaches of International Law," *Sri Lanka Guardian*, May 30, 2010. Reprinted by permission.

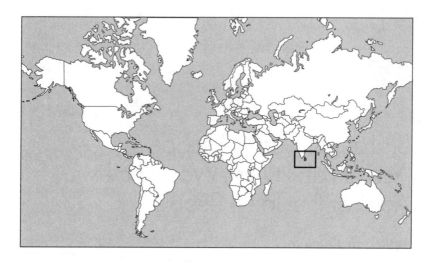

UN headquarters in New York, as well as the U.S. secretary of state, Hillary Clinton, on May 28 in Washington D.C. The learned professor also met several other U.S. politicians and downplayed the serious nature of the crimes against humanity, the war crimes, and genocide [in Sri Lanka]. He also lectured to them that insofar as the Tamils [an ethnic group in Sri Lanka] were concerned they could not have been happier.

Peiris was rushed to the U.S. within a week of the Transnational Government of Tamil Eelam (TGTE) holding its first meeting between 17 to May 18 at the historic National Constitution Center in Philadelphia, Pennsylvania, where the Constitution of the U.S was adopted in 1787. William Ramsey Clark (a former U.S. attorney general) and Domach Wal Ruach (the secretary general of Sudan People's Liberation Movement [SPLM] USA) were named as keynote speakers of the inaugural event.

At the meeting with UN's Mr. Ban was discussed the proposed visit of UN under-secretary-general for political affairs Lynn Pascoe prior to setting up a panel of experts to advise him on Sri Lanka's human rights accountability, and the entry of senior UN officials, including Mr. Pascoe.

While the professor was telling his audience that everything was hunky-dory at home, thousands of young Tamils were under detention or being killed by the Sri Lankan government. The government denies access to UN or any other foreign agencies to see the detainees. Yet, the Sri Lankan government continues to claim that they are treating the detainees humanely and after screening them releasing them. It is learnt from reliable sources that after their "release" they are paraded before the media and then again arrested.

Despite claims that the Tamils have been liberated, thousands of extra soldiers are being deployed setting up new camps in the Tamil areas, causing inconvenience and posing security threats to the civilians. The armed forces are seen wandering around the Tamil areas.

When the Tamils tried to return to their villages, particularly in the Vanni, they were sent back and disallowed to return. While it was made out that all (fictitious) land mines had been removed and all Tamils resettled, in actuality, the government is sending in hundreds of Sinhala [the majority ethnic group in Sri Lanka] families to live on Tamil properties. Despite the ongoing second-class citizen attitude, the government claims that it sees the Tamils as Sri Lankan nationals.

Don't Interfere in Our Affairs

The Sri Lankan government is trying its utmost best to step up diplomatic pressure upon the UN to abandon its proposed investigation into its conduct against the Tamils. The law professor with his previous diplomatic experience was selected primarily to rebut international accusations of human rights abuses. His mission is also to discredit the Tamil diasporas who constantly expose their misdemeanours pressuring the international community to also launch an impartial international inquiry to bring the perpetrators of war crimes to justice.

Ban Ki-Moon flew over the Vanni [an area in northern Sri Lanka] in the company of the much-despised Vijay Nambiar [an Indian diplomat and UN under-secretary-general] escorted by Sri Lankan defence officials, after the international community exerted pressure upon the UN to take immediate steps to stop the war in order to protect the remaining civilian Tamils from being massacred in the final phase of the Eelam War IV which ended May 2009.

Even after the Tamils were wantonly killed and over 300,000 "liberated" Tamils put in concentration camps in Vavuniya and kept incarcerated within razor wires, Sri Lanka did not allow access to international aid agencies nor even the UN agencies to enter to visit the displaced.

The Sri Lankan government is trying its utmost best to step up diplomatic pressure upon the UN to abandon its proposed investigation into its conduct against the Tamils.

On March 5, Secretary-General Ban told President [of Sri Lanka Mahinda] Rajapaksa that he had decided to appoint a UN panel of experts to advise him on the next steps for accountability in Sri Lanka. The Sri Lankan government responded by attacking Ban for interfering in domestic affairs, calling the inquiry panel "unwarranted" and "uncalled for." Two months later, Ban is yet to appoint members to his panel. Ban's inaction sends a signal to similar abusers announcing the appointment of farcical commissions and making loud noises seeking to block all efforts for real justice, as stated by the Human Rights Watch.

After meeting with the U.S. and UN officials, Peiris told the media that the UN panel would "have no legal and moral justification in interfering in the internal affairs of Sri Lanka as it is a sovereign state." After Ban Ki-Moon's decision to appoint a special panel on Sri Lanka, UN–Sri Lanka relations sank. After the meeting with Peiris, it is believed that top-level

UN officials were not happy with Peiris' response. He had told Mr. Ban that any international involvement would provoke a negative political reaction.

The International Crisis Group Hits at UN

A week ago the International Crisis Group (ICG), which is a think tank led by Canadian former UN war crimes prosecutor and UN High Commissioner for Human Rights Louise Arbour, said there should be international inquiry into possible war crimes which it alleged were committed by the government and the Tamil Tigers towards the close of the war. However, the Sri Lankan government continues to espouse that the army killed no civilians whatsoever, only the hardcore [Liberation Tigers of Tamil Eelam] LTTE fighters.

Arbour said the United Nations compromised its principles for a lofty goal: to preserve the ability of aid workers to provide humanitarian assistance to those in desperate need of it. But she faulted the UN's acceptance of "absolutely unacceptable" visa limitations on international staff and the UN's decision to withdraw foreign staff from the northern Sri Lankan province of Vanni in September 2008, on the eve of government forces' final offensive against the LTTE, leaving behind "very exposed" local Sri Lankan employees.

She cited the ICG's case from June 2009, in which the United Nations "was slow to react" to the abduction and torture of two UN national staff members who were detained on suspicion of collaborating with the Tamil Tigers, and "made no serious protest at their mistreatment."

Arbour said: "The UN should look at how it behaved in the whole episode.... I think it's a very sobering moment where the United Nations should reexamine the price it is willing to pay to maintain humanitarian access.... UN agencies allowed themselves to be bullied by the government and accepted a reduced role in protecting civilians, most notably with their quick acceptance of the government's September

Confronting Local Abuses Against Tamil Civilians

Human Rights Watch calls upon the Liberation Tigers of Tamil Eelam (LTTE) to:

- Stop preventing civilians from leaving areas under LTTE control. Respect the right to freedom of movement of civilians, including the right of civilians to move to government-controlled territory for safety.

- Stop all forced recruitment into the LTTE. End all abductions and coercion.

- End all recruitment of children under age 18. Cease the use of children in military operations. Release all child combatants currently in LTTE ranks, as well as all persons who were recruited when children but are now over age 18.

- Stop all abusive or unpaid forced labor, including labor characterized as "voluntary" by the LTTE. Cease demanding that all families provide labor to the LTTE. Stop forcing civilians to engage in labor directly related to the conduct of military operations, such as construction of trenches and bunkers.

- Provide humanitarian agencies and UN [United Nations] agencies safe and unhindered access to areas under LTTE control, and guarantee the security of all humanitarian and UN workers, including Vanni residents working as humanitarian or UN staff.

Human Rights Watch, Trapped and Mistreated:
LTTE Abuses Against Civilians in the Vanni,
December 15, 2008.

2008 order to remove all staff from the Vanni. . . . The Human Rights Council chose not to defend humanitarian law, but instead passed a resolution praising the conduct of the government. All of this has eroded further the standing of the UN in Sri Lanka and elsewhere."

She also criticized Ban for meeting with President Rajapaksa and failing to press for an independent investigation.

Channel 4 News Releases New Torture Video Evidence

Britain's leading BBC Channel 4 News carried new video evidence. A senior Sri Lankan army commander and frontline soldier told Channel 4 News that point-blank executions of Tamils at the end of the Sri Lankan civil war were carried out under orders.

Earlier, in August 2009, Channel 4 News obtained video evidence, later authenticated by the United Nations, purporting to show point-blank executions of Tamils by uniformed Sri Lankan soldiers. Now, a senior army commander and a frontline soldier have told Channel 4 News that such killings were indeed ordered from the top. One frontline soldier said: "Yes, our commander ordered us to kill everyone. We killed everyone." The army commander said: "Definitely, the order would have been to kill everybody and finish them off. . . . I don't think we wanted to keep any hardcore elements, so they were done away with. It is clear that such orders were, in fact, received from the top."

The Human Rights Watch [HRW] issued a statement on May 20 titled "Sri Lanka: New Evidence of Wartime Abuses" which said: "New evidence of wartime abuses by Sri Lankan government forces and the separatist Liberation Tigers of Tamil Eelam (LTTE) during the armed conflict that ended one year ago demonstrates the need for an independent international investigation into violations of the laws of war."

The Human Rights Watch has examined more than 200 photos taken on the front lines in early 2009 by a soldier from the Sri Lankan Air Mobile Brigade. Among these are a series of five photos showing a man who appears to have been captured by the Sri Lankan army. An independent source identified the man by name and told the Human Rights Watch that he was a long-term member of the LTTE's political wing from Jaffna.

Despite allegations of war crimes, Sri Lanka's government has managed to avoid an independent inquiry. But the evidence continues to mount.

While the Human Rights Watch cannot conclusively determine that the man was summarily executed in custody, the available evidence indicates that a full investigation is warranted. Several of the photos also show what appear to be dead women in LTTE uniforms with their shirts pulled up and their pants pulled down, raising concerns that they might have been sexually abused or their corpses mutilated. Again, such evidence is not conclusive but shows the need for an investigation.

The HRW further said: "Sri Lanka has a long history of establishing ad hoc commissions to deflect international criticism over its poor human rights record and widespread impunity.... Since independence in 1948, Sri Lanka has established at least nine such commissions, none of which have produced any significant results."

Despite allegations of war crimes, Sri Lanka's government has managed to avoid an independent inquiry. But the evidence continues to mount. Sri Lanka is doing its best to exert pressure upon the UN and other leading global powers which were openly vocal demanding international investigation, including the U.S., to give up their demands to punish Sri Lanka. Rather, Sri Lanka is expecting the global powers to forget and forgive the past, and inviting the international community to do business with Sri Lanka. As a tiny island in the Indian Ocean, Sri Lanka is a real security threat to the global stability. This proves by way of how the Sri Lankan leaders and diplomats are treating the world when the responsible world organizations are oblique to do their duties.

Developing Countries Have a Poor Record on Gay Rights

The Economist

The Economist *is a weekly news and international affairs magazine. In the following viewpoint, the author considers the harsh laws that many developing countries are passing against homosexuality. Not only are these laws intolerant, the* Economist *maintains, but they may also threaten the public health in these countries—particularly by obstructing the ongoing fight against HIV/AIDS.*

As you read, consider the following questions:

1. What sentence did a court in Malawi impose on Steven Monjeza and Tiwonge Chimbalanga?
2. How many countries criminalize homosexual sex, according to the viewpoint?
3. Which country was the first to ban homophobic discrimination in its constitution?

Their crimes were "gross indecency" and "unnatural acts". Their sentence was 14 years' hard labour: one intended, said the judge, to scare others. He has succeeded. A court in Malawi last week [in May 2010] horrified many with its treatment of Steven Monjeza and Tiwonge Chimbalanga, a gay

The Economist, "A Well-Locked Closet," *The Economist*, May 27, 2010. Reprinted by permission.

couple engaged to be married. The two men are the latest victims of a crackdown on gay rights in much of the developing world, particularly Africa.

Some 80 countries criminalise consensual homosexual sex. Over half rely on "sodomy" laws left over from British colonialism. But many are trying to make their laws even more repressive. Last year, Burundi's president, Pierre Nkurunziza, signed a law criminalising consensual gay sex, despite the Senate's overwhelming rejection of the bill. A draconian bill proposed in Uganda would dole out jail sentences for failing to report gay people to the police and could impose the death penalty for gay sex if one of the participants is HIV positive. In March Zimbabwe's president, Robert Mugabe, who once described gay people as worse than dogs or pigs, ruled out constitutional changes outlawing discrimination based on sexual orientation.

Blaming the West

In many former colonies, denouncing homosexuality as an "unAfrican" Western import has become an easy way for politicians to boost both their popularity and their nationalist credentials. But Peter Tatchell, a veteran gay rights campaigner, says the real import into Africa is not homosexuality but politicised homophobia.

This has, he argues, coincided with an influx of conservative Christians, mainly from America, who are eager to engage African clergy in their own domestic battle against homosexuality. David Bahati, the Ugandan MP [member of Parliament] who proposed its horrid bill, is a member of the Fellowship, a conservative American religious and political organisation. "Africa must seem an exciting place for evangelical Christians from places like America," says Marc Epprecht, a Canadian academic who studies homosexuality in Africa. "They can make much bigger gains in their culture wars there than they can in their own countries." Their ideas have found fertile ground. In May this year, George Kunda, Zambia's vice president, lambasted gay people, saying they undermined the country's Christian values and that sadism and Satanism could be the result.

How countries treat one particularly vulnerable group is a good measure of how they will act towards the rest of their citizens.

The Dangers of a Homosexual Witch Hunt

Discrimination against gays, in Africa in particular, risks undermining the fight against HIV/AIDS. In February, those suspected of being gay were targeted in Kenya in mob violence at a government health centre providing HIV/AIDS services. Bishop Joshua Banda, chairman of Zambia's National AIDS Council, said that donor countries' efforts to speak out against violations of gay rights were against Zambia's "traditional values". The increasing crackdown on gay rights in Africa will be a disaster for public health, according to Mr Epprecht, as gay people go underground and do not get treatment for HIV/AIDS.

The problem goes beyond Africa and is more than one of state-sponsored homophobia. In Iraq, for example, homosexuality is legal. But in 2009 Human Rights Watch described the persecution that men suspected of being gay there face, including kidnappings, rape, torture and extrajudicial killings. In the aftermath of the 2003 invasion [of Iraq], there has been a growing fear of the "feminisation" of Iraqi men. The Mahdi Army, a Shia militia, has played on these fears and, claiming to uphold religious values and morality, offered violent "solutions". Members of the Iraqi security forces have also been accused of colluding in the violence.

The Global Picture for Gays and Lesbians

Country	Status	Penalty or social sanctions
Iran	Illegal	Death for men; 100 lashes for women, death on fourth conviction
Nigeria	Male illegal; both illegal in areas under *sharia* law	*Sharia* areas: up to death for men, up to 50 lashes and six months in prison for women; for men elsewhere, up to 14 years in prison
Afghanistan	Illegal	Maximum of death penalty; no known cases of death sentences since the end of Taliban rule
Uganda	Illegal	Up to life prison sentence*
Malawi	Male illegal	Up to 14 years in prison, with or without corporal punishment
Malaysia	Illegal	Fine, prison sentence two to 20 years, whippings
Jamaica	Male illegal	Prison and hard labour for up to ten years
Zimbabwe	Male illegal	Fine, up to a year in prison
Morocco	Illegal	Fine, six months to three years in prison
Lebanon	Illegal	Up to a year in prison
Iraq	Not illegal	Extrajudicial executions, kidnappings, torture, rape
South Africa	Legal since 1994	Beatings, rape, murder

*Bill proposed in October 2009 would introduce the death penalty

TAKEN FROM: International Lesbian, Gay, Bisexual, Trans and Intersex Association; "A Well-Locked Closet," *The Economist*, May 27, 2010.

The Case of Eudy Simelane

South Africa was the first country anywhere to ban homophobic discrimination in its constitution. It is the only country in Africa to allow gay marriage. In formal legal terms, it is a beacon for gay rights, says Mr Tatchell. But the growing phenomenon of "corrective rape" both there and in Zimbabwe, where women are assaulted in an attempt to "cure" them of lesbianism, suggests these laws often fail on the ground. As worrying to campaigners as the violence itself is a reluctance by the authorities to acknowledge that the attacks are motivated by homophobia. In April 2008 Eudy Simelane, a South African football player who was a lesbian, was gang-raped and stabbed to death. Two men were convicted of her murder but, in his sentencing, the judge denied that Ms Simelane's sexuality played a part in the crime.

Hopes rose a little in June 2009 when India overturned its 149-year-old sodomy law but since then the global trend seems to have been in the opposite direction. Campaigners argue the proposed laws have implications beyond gay rights. How countries treat one particularly vulnerable group is a good measure of how they will act towards the rest of their citizens.

Periodical and Internet Sources Bibliography

The following articles have been selected to supplement the diverse views presented in this chapter.

Ahmednasir Abdullahi	"For the West, Human Rights No Longer Universal," *Daily Nation* (Kenya), September 18, 2010.
John Baglow	"A Circus of Nationalists," *National Post* (Canada), December 24, 2009.
BBC News	"EU Nations and Roma Repatriation," September 17, 2010.
Jennifer Brown	"Pride Toronto Fights for Queer Rights Around the World," *Toronto Star*, June 25, 2010.
Edward Ellis	"Venezuela Should Follow Argentina's Example on Gay Rights," Venezuelaanalysis.com, July 16, 2010. http://venezuelaanalysis.com.
Guadalajara Reporter	"Supreme Court Ruling Is Welcomed by Gay Community," August 13, 2010.
Olivia Miljanic and Robert Zaretsky	"France: Behind the Expulsion of the Roma," *Le Monde diplomatique* (Paris, France), September 3, 2010.
Abdulkadir Badsha Mukhtar	"Rights Group Wants Amnesty for Boko Haram Followers," *Daily Trust* (Nigeria), October 12, 2010.
Abdullah S. al-Shehri	"New Controversy for Building a Mosque, but This Time in France," *Saudi Gazette*, October 12, 2010.
Gregory Theintz	"Colombia: Liberal in Theory, Homophobic in Practice," *Colombia Reports*, April 30, 2010.

GLOBALVIEWPOINTS

CHAPTER 4

Human
Rights Challenges

Chad Has a Problem with Violence Against Women

IRIN

IRIN, or the Integrated Regional Information Networks, is a United Nations news agency that focuses on humanitarian stories in underreported and developing regions. In the following viewpoint, the agency reports that there is a growing movement to strengthen domestic violence laws and fight the prevailing cultural acceptance of violence against women.

As you read, consider the following questions:

1. What event happened in December 2008 that was the first of its kind in Guelendeng?
2. How does the president of APLFT describe existing legal remedies to protect women against domestic violence?
3. What do human rights activists feel is critical to protecting women's rights?

Awa was killed by her husband last November [2008] in Guelendeng, 150km [kilometers] south of the Chad capital N'djamena. Her death was the tipping point for the town's women, who, appalled by the rampant violence they face, have decided to fight for their rights.

In December dozens of women took part in a protest march, the first of its kind in Guelendeng, to condemn the

IRIN, "Chad Fighting Violence Against Women—but How?" IRINNews.org, April 3, 2009. Reprinted by permission.

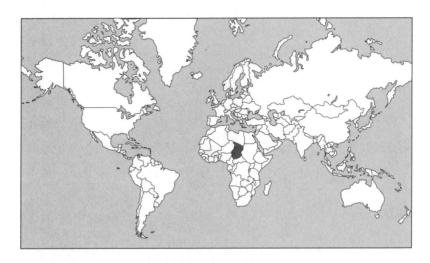

violation of their rights and to call the government to account over the impunity that prevails.

Murders, beatings, underage marriage, sexual violence—the list of violations is long. "There have been so many cases of violence that we can no longer sit and do nothing," Catherine Ndaokaï, information and awareness officer for the Violence Against Women Monitoring Committee, told IRIN [Integrated Regional Information Networks]. "This violence is so widespread that men even sit around and chat about it."

Involvement in the march posed a threat for many participants, said Martine Klah, president of the monitoring committee that was created the day after the march "so that the movement does not stop here".

The prevailing context of violence in a country where attacks on civilians by armed groups and general instability have been the norm for decades has undoubtedly exacerbated violence against women.

In this region where men are traditionally seen as the "dominant ones", Klah said, "Men told us that they were going to kill us one by one for having held that march."

Cultural beliefs constitute one of the greatest obstacles to fighting the violence, the women said. "Women are at the bottom of the [social] ladder and are seen as property", said Delphine Kemneloum Djiraibe, national coordinator of the monitoring committee to Call for Peace and National Reconciliation in Chad. "People can do whatever they want to a woman."

The prevailing context of violence in a country where attacks on civilians by armed groups and general instability have been the norm for decades has undoubtedly exacerbated violence against women, human rights activists say.

"Men say that women are behind the [violent attacks], but back in the time of our grandparents, people did not kill each other," information officer Ndaokaï said. "Even if a woman was caught [doing something wrong], a man would have just got rid of her."

Legal Gaps and Cultural Obstacles

The women of Guelendeng recognise there is a lack of support for victims of abuse. "We don't know the basic legal documentation to defend the rights of women," monitoring committee president Klah said.

Chad has laws on the books, including on reproductive health, but the implementing decrees were never published, rights activists say. A family code bill, drawn up several years ago still has not gone through Parliament. Human rights activists say the delay is due to conservatives who think the law gives women too much power.

In the meantime magistrates are attempting to use existing documentation from the penal code, such as sections relating to 'bodily harm', Lydie Asngar Mbaiassem Latoï, director of the promotion of women and gender integration unit at the Ministry of Social Affairs, told IRIN.

But existing legal remedies are inadequate, women say. The gaps and the prevailing tendency for impunity mean that the perpetrators of this violence are almost never prosecuted—

and men know this, which encourages them to continue these acts, Larlem Marie, president of APLFT, an organization promoting basic rights in Chad, told IRIN.

"Recently a man who wanted to attack his wife told her he could kill her because either way he would get away with it," Larlem said. "He pointed to a case in which a man killed his wife without the slightest repercussion," she told IRIN.

Women often fail to file a complaint because they are terrified of retaliation. Djiraibe pointed out that even were a woman to pursue a case, she would have nowhere to go to be safe from her attacker, as no facilities are available for victims of violence, particularly domestic violence.

"There is opposition to [creating facilities of this kind] on the grounds that it encourages women to leave their homes," she said. "So there is no alternative [to the conjugal home]; if women [lodge a complaint] they will end up on the streets."

Were a woman to pursue a [legal] case, she would have nowhere to go to be safe from her attacker, as no facilities are available for victims of violence.

Widespread Violence Must Be Confronted

While Guelendeng's women are speaking out, many more women around the country suffer in silence, rights activists say. Humanitarian and human rights organisations report that the phenomenon is widespread but a lack of studies makes it difficult to determine the extent.

The Social Affairs Ministry plans to launch a nationwide survey this year [2009] that will in part measure the extent of violence against women, with support from UNFPA [the United Nations Population Fund], according to Mbaiassem Latoï. And the ministry and UNFPA are working on a free help line connected to the police, aimed at giving victims legal and medical help.

One Woman's Story

When Habiba was 12 her deceased father's brother gave her away to be married to a military officer in his 50s. She became his third wife and gave birth to a son the following year. Habiba, who said her husband regularly beats her, has run away from the family home in [Chad's capital city] N'djamena several times to seek refuge with her mother in Guelendeng, a town 150km [kilometers] away. But her uncle has sent her back to her husband each time. During one of her last escape attempts . . . her husband tried to kill her.

"It was around 7 P.M. when he arrived [in Guelendeng] and found me at the side of the road. He told me he had just come to kill me and go. Then he stabbed me twice in the back," said Habiba, who is alive only because passersby intervened.

The regional prefect, Gabdibe Passore Ouadjiri Loth, was alerted to the situation by human rights organisations and women's groups in Guelendeng and he intervened.

"I tried to get the parents, the husband, [local and traditional] chiefs and the young girl together," he told IRIN [the Integrated Regional Information Networks]. "We organised four meetings but the husband refused to come."

According to human rights defenders, the husband, who was released after what one referred to as "a so-called arrest" in N'djamena, continues to make death threats to Habiba.

IRIN, "Chad: Fighting Violence Against Women—but How?"
IRINNews.org, April 3, 2009. www.irinnews.org.

Aid workers say it is an issue that demands immediate action. "There is no sense of urgency even though we are facing a growing level of violence and there are more and more reports of feelings of insecurity," said Marzio Babille, UN [United Nations] Children's Fund (UNICEF) representative in Chad.

Human rights activists say support from the authorities is critical to protecting women's rights. The women of Guelendeng said they are fortunate in this respect. "We can go and see the [regional] prefect if we have a problem; he listens to us and supports us," said one of the women.

Gabdibe Passore Ouadjiri Loth, the prefect, has been involved in several human rights cases and has links with the Ministry of the Interior and the presidency. "If a man will not protect his own mother, whom will he protect?" he said. But he recognised that the country was still run by "male chauvinists".

The Ministry of Social Affairs Mbaiassem Latoï said: "Things are moving forward slowly but surely. Everything is under construction: laws, policies."

She added: "The [economic and security] crisis has turned everything upside down: Many women have become heads of households and men are realising that they should not neglect them. This awakening has not reached its peak, but it will come. Either way, civil society will not stop."

Saudi Arabia Must Address the Issue of Male Guardianship

Christoph Wilcke

Christoph Wilcke is a senior Middle East researcher for Human Rights Watch. In the following viewpoint, he points out that although Saudi Arabia's Human Rights Commission stated it would abolish the practice of male guardianship over women's lives, it has failed to do so. Wilcke argues that the rights of Saudi women are still being violated by this antiquated system.

As you read, consider the following questions:

1. In Wilcke's view, how did Ahmed al-Ghamdi cause a stir in 2010?

2. Why was Sawsan Salim sentenced to three hundred lashes and one and a half years in prison in January 2010?

3. What does a strict labor law passed in 2005 require of women?

Ahmed al-Ghamdi, the chief of the religious police in Mecca, caused a stir earlier this year [2010] when he declared that there were no Islamic texts prohibiting the innocent mingling of men and women. The national head of the religious police duly sacked Ghamdi in April, but he was reinstated, reportedly on orders from very high authority.

Christoph Wilcke, "Still Waiting for Saudi Arabia," *Jerusalem Post*, May 15, 2010. Reprinted by permission.

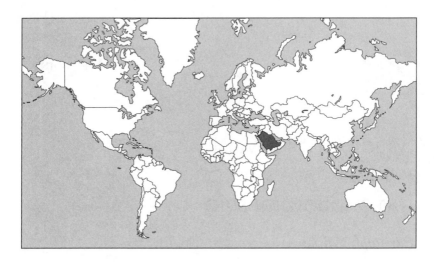

Some in the kingdom saw the Ghamdi affair as opening the gates to debauchery, while others thought it a milestone in the struggle for women's rights. King Abdullah [of Saudi Arabia] has cautiously but consistently promoted loosening the rigid segregation of men and women practiced in the kingdom.

All Talk, No Action

However, he has done nothing to loosen the stringent ties that hobble women's most basic rights. The root problem is not segregation as such, but the system of male guardianship: Male relatives can and routinely do dictate a woman's everyday decisions—to leave the house to shop or study or visit a government office, for example—as though she were a child.

In June 2009, Bandar al-Aiban, the head of the government's Human Rights Commission, accepted the recommendation of the UN [United Nations] Human Rights Council to abolish this system of male guardianship, put to Saudi Arabia during the council's comprehensive review of the kingdom's human rights record. The commission noted that guardianship can lead to coercion, saying, "There are no statutory requirements that necessitate guardianship . . . and the Shari'a notion of the tutelage link [guardianship] between men and women is not a legal stipulation."

But it appears that nothing has changed in practice. Many Saudi government and private hospitals still require a woman's male guardian to sign a consent form for her to undergo a medical procedure. I recently spoke with a woman who was desperate because her husband was in incommunicado [without communication] detention and thus could not sign the required consent form for her to get treatment. After weeks, the authorities allowed her to visit him, obtain the form and finally have the operation.

The Role of Guardians

Guardians—a father, husband, brother or even a divorced woman's son—must also approve a woman's foreign or domestic travel. In one current case, Nazia Quazi, a 24-year-old dual Indian and Canadian citizen, has only just left Saudi Arabia after being stuck there for three years. Her father lured her to Saudi Arabia, where he lives, and refused to grant her permission to leave. Saudi authorities acquiesced in preventing her from returning home to Canada.

In January, a court sentenced Sawsan Salim, a naturalized Saudi citizen living in the conservative Qasim area, to 300 lashes and one and a half years in prison, where she remains, because she addressed government officials without a male guardian.

In March, *Al-Hayat* wrote about a Saudi female student who had to give up her government scholarship for a doctorate abroad after she sent her teenage nephew back to Saudi Arabia because he stopped going to school and began drinking. He was the male guardian whom the Ministry of Higher Education had required to accompany her.

What Is Male Guardianship?

The Saudi government has instituted a system whereby every Saudi woman must have a male guardian, normally a father or husband, who is tasked with making a range of critical decisions on her behalf. This policy, grounded in the most restrictive interpretation of an ambiguous Quranic verse, is the most significant impediment to the realization of women's rights in the kingdom. The Saudi authorities essentially treat adult women like legal minors who are entitled to little authority over their own lives and well-being.

Every Saudi woman, regardless of her economic or social status, is affected by these guardianship policies and the deprivation of rights that their enforcement entails. Adult women generally must obtain permission from a guardian to work, travel, study, or marry. Saudi women are similarly denied the right to make even the most trivial decisions on behalf of their children.

Male guardianship over adult women also contributes to their risk of confronting family violence and makes it nearly impossible for survivors of family violence to avail themselves of protection or redress mechanisms. Social workers, physicians, and lawyers told Human Rights Watch about the near impossibility of removing male guardianship of women and children, even from abusive male guardians.

Human Rights Watch,
"Perpetual Minors," April 19, 2008.

Improvements in Women's Rights Are Symbolic

There have been some improvements for women, but they have been mostly symbolic, like the appointment last year of a woman as a deputy minister or the appointment of six female consultants to the appointed all-male Shura Council, which has some of the functions of a parliament.

The new King Abdullah University of Science and Technology allows men and women to mix on campus, but few Saudis study there. Over the past years, women have been admitted in the kingdom to study law and engineering, previously off-limits to women, and a promised law would allow women lawyers to litigate in court in certain cases, but their ability to practice law will continue to depend on the consent of male guardians.

The 2005 labor law continues to require strict gender segregation at the workplace, making it difficult for law firms to hire female lawyers because they have to create separate offices. The Human Rights Commission until recently did not have a women's department because, its board members told Human Rights Watch, there were no separate toilet facilities.

No woman should have to get a guardian's consent to approach a government office, to get medical care or a job, or to go to school or to travel.

Saudi schools, unfortunately, still reinforce the culture of guardianship. A high school textbook on Islamic culture, for example, in a chapter on the rights of wives, states that "it is the nature of the woman to be weak, and if she were left without being taken by the hand, she would corrupt and become corrupted."

Badria al-Bishr, writing in March in *Al-Hayat* against the notions underlying guardianship, put it this way: "Frankly, I say that if those words were said to me in a public place, I would think that someone was insulting me."

Saudi authorities should end male guardianship over women. No woman should have to get a guardian's consent to approach a government office, to get medical care or a job, or to go to school or to travel. The Saudi government has promised to end this system. It should keep that promise.

Sudan's Merowe Dam Has Sparked Several Human Rights Abuses

Adrian Kriesch

Adrian Kriesch is a reporter for Deutsche Welle, *Germany's international broadcaster. In the following viewpoint, he details some of the damage caused by the construction of the Merowe Dam in northern Sudan, including the flooding of historical sites and the displacement of thousands of people. Kriesch argues that there has to be a consideration for human rights in large government projects.*

As you read, consider the following questions:

1. What is the electricity production capacity of the Merowe Dam?
2. According to charges by the European Center for Constitutional and Human Rights, how many families were displaced by the Merowe Dam project?
3. How many more Sudanese will be displaced by future dam projects, in Kriesch's estimation?

With an electricity production capacity of 1250 megawatts, the Merowe Dam is Africa's largest hydroelectric project. The dam on the Nile River in northern Sudan was designed to provide power and water for farming to the entire country.

Adrian Kriesch, "Controversial Sudanese Dam Sparks Human Rights Complaint," *Deutsche Welle*, May 19, 2010. Reprinted by permission.

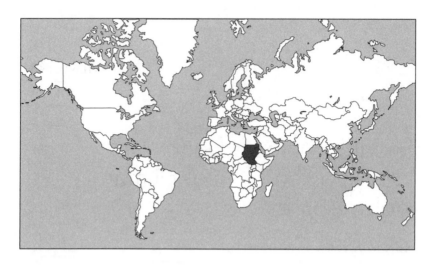

But the large-scale project has also had a significant impact on the community. Historical sites were flooded, and thousands of people were reportedly forced to flee their homes.

In 2007, UN special rapporteur on adequate housing Miloon Kothari responded to "numerous reports of violations of civil and political rights" by calling for suspension of the Merowe Dam's construction until an independent evaluation could be conducted.

Alleged failure to comply with international guidelines on evicting residents near the project has prompted one human rights group to take action.

The Berlin-based European Center for Constitutional and Human Rights filed a criminal complaint earlier this month against one of the firms involved in the project, Lahmeyer International, based in Bad Vilbel near Frankfurt. The company has denied any wrongdoing.

The ECCHR charges that the company was involved in the flooding of 30 villages and the forced displacement of more than 4,700 families in the region near the dam in northern Sudan.

A Local Voice Speaks Out

The area around the Merowe Dam is now cordoned off and Sudan's government has allegedly barred journalists from accessing the site.

Anyone who publicly opposes the project and the forced relocations due to the dam become potential targets for harassment. What started as peaceful protests by local residents in previous years reportedly turned violent, ending in the shooting and arrest of demonstrators by Sudanese security forces.

Despite the risks, Ali Askouri, a native of the region near the dam and community representative, refuses to be intimidated. He has since moved to London, but Askouri frequently visits his family in Sudan—and has a firsthand perspective of the project's impact.

"It's a complete disaster," he said. "All (residents') farming land is gone, all their crops are gone; they lost their animals, they lost their harvests." Askouri said some villages were completely flooded, and families became divided over whether to stay or go.

His was among those families separated by construction of the dam. While some of Askouri's relatives relocated to the hillside, which wasn't affected by floodwaters, others moved to a plot of barren land which the Sudanese government provided the family as compensation.

Legal Action

Askouri had little faith that pressuring the Sudanese government would deliver any progress. So he opted to join forces with the ECCHR in Germany. Together, they're challenging one of the companies involved in the dam's construction and have filed a criminal complaint against two of their executive employees.

Lahmeyer International was the engineering firm in charge of planning and supervising the Merowe Dam project. In 2006 and 2008, two areas behind the dam were flooded—but according to human rights advocates, Lahmeyer employees knew that thousands of people were still living there.

"Lahmeyer began construction even though the resettlement plans had not been fully negotiated with the affected population—as demanded by international World Bank standards," the ECCHR's website stated.

The organization alleged that the company's personnel did not inform residents ahead of the flooding, forcing them to flee almost empty-handed. Many of them lost everything they owned.

"With these kinds of dam projects, it's important to have cooperation and participation with the local population," said Ulrich Delius, Africa consultant for the Society for Threatened Peoples.

"And here, the participation was such that 90 percent of the local population demonstrated against it, these demonstrations are quelled with armed violence and people get arrested."

"You just can't say there was any participation in the planning," he added.

The Merowe project has the potential to boost prosperity in Sudan, but it leaves behind a troubling legacy.

Allegations Denied

Lahmeyer International has rejected all claims made against the company.

Although it declined to be interviewed by Deutsche Welle, Egon Failer, one of the company's dam construction managers, told German news magazine *Der Spiegel* that "residents were given due notice" of the construction plans.

"Consultants spent years conducting surveys and discussions in the villages and even counted the date trees to tally up compensations."

It's not the first time the company has faced challenges on its overseas projects. In 2006, the World Bank sanctioned Lahmeyer International for its role in a corruption scandal connected with a project in Lesotho. The company was barred from receiving World Bank–funded contracts for seven years.

The Sudanese government said the Merowe Dam would supply enough power to meet the entire population's energy needs. But even more dams are slated for construction in the country—meaning that another 175,000 people could face displacement from their homes. In addition, Lahmeyer International is involved in at least one of the future projects.

"If the company insists on going into other projects, that means the company has no respect for human rights," local community representative Ali Askouri said. "They have had the experience—how can you go into another project with the same government, with the same group of officials, who pay no attention whatsoever to the rights of the affected communities?"

The Merowe project has the potential to boost prosperity in Sudan, but it leaves behind a troubling legacy. Human rights advocates hope the current complaint will set a new precedent for how companies approach human rights issues.

Africa Must Rely on the International Criminal Court to Address Human Rights Violations

Olivier Kambala wa Kambala

Olivier Kambala wa Kambala is a Congolese human rights law-yer. In the following viewpoint, he contends that the International Criminal Court (ICC) is the only option for people in some African countries that lack a national initiative to prosecute war crimes, genocide, and other violations of human rights. To be effective, the ICC must find a practical approach to its basic mission.

As you read, consider the following questions:

1. What role did the Democratic Republic of the Congo (DRC) have in establishing the ICC?

2. How is the ICC subject to international politics, according to the author?

3. How are civic groups in South Africa testing that country's law in regard to crimes in Zimbabwe?

A frican countries comprise one of the largest blocs of sig-natories to the International Criminal Court (ICC) and are critical actors in the institution, but their role is often

Olivier Kambala wa Kambala, "Africa: Victims of Rights Violations Turn Their Eyes to Kampala," allAfrica.com, May 29, 2010. Reprinted by permission of the author.

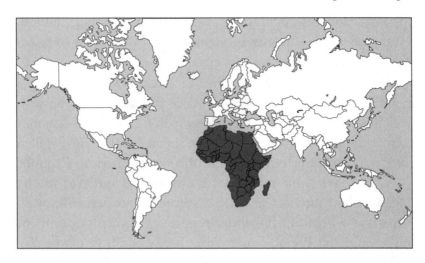

overlooked. In fact, it was the Democratic Republic of the Congo's (DRC's) ratification of the Rome Statute [of the International Criminal Court] in 2002 that officially established the ICC—an institution impossible to envision 50 years earlier.

Coincidentally, the DRC is also the country in which the ICC put an end to what was beginning to appear as reluctance to act on the part of the international community to deal with suspected war criminals.

All four occupants of the ICC's Scheveningen detention centre in the Netherlands are Congolese: Thomas Lubanga, Mathieu Ngudjolo Chui, Germain Katanga and Jean-Pierre Bemba Gombo. The first cases to be heard at the ICC focus on war crimes and crimes against humanity committed in the DRC and the Central African Republic. So it is not an overstatement to say that the construction of international criminal justice has crossed the Rubicon [meaning passing the point of no return] in Africa: *alea jacta est*—The Die is Cast!

The Challenges to the ICC in Africa

Meanwhile, the challenges the ICC faces in Africa are manifold.

First, the ICC's operation is anchored in ongoing conflicts. Four of five African cases brought before the court involve active insurrections.

The DRC has been in upheaval since 1996, marked by a reprehensible pattern of sexual violence. Uganda's battle with [religious and military leader] Joseph Kony's Lord's Resistance Army [LRA] has affected not only Sudan but has now spilled over into northwestern DRC and the Central African Republic (CAR). Apart from reaping the bitter consequences of the LRA's violent tactics, the CAR is still in a "no peace, no war" situation, with fresh hostilities reported between government forces and the Popular Army for the Restoration of the Republic and Democracy in the north, and Sudan's Darfur region is not yet at peace.

Such contexts complicate the ICC prosecutor's work. On the one hand he possesses an irrevocable mandate to investigate cases and seek indictments. On the other, he has to juggle with that the severe consequences that the exercise of his mandate may cause to vulnerable civilians bearing the brunt of hostilities. Regardless of the nature of the risks, whether hypothetical or real, the prosecutor finds himself in situations where national politics influence his power.

International Politics Is a Complication

The ICC prosecutor is also subject to international politics, which can dictate the freezing of proceedings for a year at a time through the United Nations Security Council. The process is also subject to his own political assessment of the interests of justice.

The situation in Sudan sparked controversy over the Security Council's power to defer charges against Sudan's President Omar al-Bashir for war crimes and crimes against humanity. Sudan is not a state party to the Rome Statute and al-Bashir is a sitting head of state—two factors that heightened tension between the African Union and the ICC.

Whether or not ICC prosecution can fuel or re-ignite a conflict is debatable.

The arrest of Jean-Pierre Bemba, former vice president of the DRC and one of the front-runners in its 2006 presidential elections, did not result in the significant instability that many expected. Perhaps the defeat of Bemba's remnant elite forces in March 2007 before his "exfiltration" to Portugal helped assuage violence. Meanwhile, DRC authorities have raised the spectre of renewed instability in the country's east if the arrest warrant against General Bosco Ntanganda were to be enforced.

In the Ituri district however, followers of Thomas Lubanga, Mathieu Ngudjolo and Germain Katanga did not use the arrest and transfer of their leaders to The Hague as a new *casus belli* [justification for acts of war]. The trio was already in the custody of the Congolese government when the ICC arrest warrants were issued, which could be read as an inhibiting factor. But any deterrent effect of their removals is largely hypothetical.

Perhaps in the end, it is possible that the ICC is a reality impacting on African conflict.

The Case of Uganda

In Uganda, the indictment of top leaders of the LRA, together with the changing situation in South Sudan, softened the movement's stance, leading to their participation in the Juba peace negotiations, before it hardened again. Since its refusal to sign the final peace deal brokered in Juba in 2008, the LRA has been conducting a terror campaign against populations of northeastern DRC and southern Central African Republic, according to human rights groups. The massacre in Doruma in the DRC in December 2008 was the climax of the LRA's revived military activities.

Why Are So Many ICC Cases in Africa?

The prosecutor of the ICC [International Criminal Court] has encouraged self-referrals, and the only such referrals have been from African countries. While the ICC has received some 1,700 communications to investigate alleged crimes in 139 countries, 80 percent of these communications have been found outside the jurisdiction of the court. This is "not a question of picking on Africa," says John Washburn of the American NGO [nongovernmental organization] Coalition for the ICC. "The UN [United Nations] Security Council referred [Darfur], and the other countries came forward voluntarily."

Stephanie Hanson,
"Africa and the International Criminal Court,"
Council on Foreign Relations, July 24, 2008.

In Guinea-Conakry, it is arguable that the statement of the Office of the Prosecutor that it would test whether the 28 September 2009 massacres were admissible before the court, prompted the junta to allow an international commission of inquiry.

Perhaps in the end, it is possible that the ICC is a reality impacting on African conflict. And this alone is an important milestone in 21st-century conflict-resolution practices.

The ICC Should Not Be the First Option

The recourse to the ICC as the channel of first preference to remedy the gross violation of human rights in the five situations before the court contradicts to some extent the mind-set of the drafters of the Rome Statute. They believed preference should be given to national courts, and the ICC's jurisdiction should be complementary to national efforts. Only in situations of state unwillingness and inability to investigate and prosecute would ICC proceedings take precedence.

Four of the five situations before the ICC have been referred by states. Few referring states have effectively enacted complementary provisions in their national legislation. In fact, only five African countries—Senegal, South Africa, Mali, Kenya and most recently Uganda—have passed domestic legislation relating to the Rome Statute.

The creation of real space on the African continent which is hostile to impunity for perpetrators will depend on the number of states implementing legislation that complements the statute. Those laws are necessary tools to bring about judicial cooperation between both the ICC and African countries on the one hand, and between African countries themselves on the other.

Most importantly, by turning to the Rome Statute's standards, implementing countries will be able to hold trials at home, based on international criminal standards laid down by the statute.

South Africa Tests Law

In South Africa, civic groups are testing the implementation of that country's 2002 law . . . to bring to account Zimbabwean officials alleged to be responsible for mass torture in Zimbabwe. The South African act grants jurisdiction to South African courts, in this particular case, if the alleged perpetrator is apprehended on South African territory.

This is an illustration of how the limited but useful jurisdiction stemming from the Rome Statute's domestication could potentially work. Widely implemented, it could result in proper universal jurisdiction to prosecute war crimes, crimes against humanity and genocide. But we cannot begin to contemplate such a situation if African countries that have referred situations to the ICC fail to take steps to domesticate the statute.

In another area, the ICC should consider playing a role in national prosecutorial initiatives based on the provisions of the Rome Statute. This scenario would apply to countries unilaterally applying the Rome Statute to domestic prosecutions, in the absence of enacting measures.

The DRC's military courts—which possess exclusive jurisdiction over war crimes, crimes against humanity and genocide—initiated a series of trials in 2006 and 2007, invoking the Rome Statute as the basis of prosecution. In the absence of ICC implementing legislation, these courts proceeded and rendered verdicts, with compensatory provisions for the victims. In addition to these trials, the defunct military structures of the Movement for the Liberation of the Congo (MLC) of Jean-Pierre Bemba claimed to have conducted trials of fighters accused of "crimes of rape, pillaging and murder" in 2002.

The ICC has an opportunity and a legal obligation to play a role in analysing the military courts' proceedings and decisions. For the Congolese victims, it could be useful for the ICC's Trust Fund for Victims to begin to assist in providing the reparations ordered by Congolese courts. In the midst of criticism that the ICC interferes in domestic affairs, the court could demonstrate that it can be as useful in the DRC as in The Hague.

Africa Needs an Effective and Just ICC

Africans, especially victims of gross human rights violations who are mostly denied justice in their respective countries, are watching the ICC. Sceptical or enthusiastic, resistant or converted to the cause of international justice, the elites or the masses, Africans expect the ICC to curb endemic manifestations of gross human rights violations.

In the meantime, the configurations of the ICC mandate can only allow precedent setting in terms of fair and impartial trials, victims' participation and compensation. Those standards are then expected to reverberate in domestic proceedings.

The direction the ICC takes in Africa will depend on its ability to . . . balance expectations and reality and begin to play an important role in the prevention and repression of mass atrocities.

The ICC also has an opportunity to impress upon the collective memory of Africans that such crimes have been dealt with efficiently, reducing their chances of recurring.

In the absence of national initiatives to establish the truth and bring perpetrators to account, the ICC is currently the only available option for most victims. The direction the ICC takes in Africa will depend on its ability to rise from poor beginnings, hampered by inappropriate and often uninformed criticism, to balance expectations and reality and begin to play an important role in the prevention and repression of mass atrocities.

Haiti's Human Rights Challenges

Amnesty International

Amnesty International is an international nongovernmental organization that aims to address human rights abuses all over the world and advocate for the human rights of all people. In the following viewpoint, Amnesty International discusses a number of major human rights challenges that face Haiti after the devastating earthquake that hit in 2010. These challenges include the exploitation of children, establishing security, protecting the displaced and the rights of women, and ensuring the accountability of international forces working in Haiti.

As you read, consider the following questions:

1. How does Amnesty International think that children can be exploited?
2. What should be one of Haiti's top priorities, according to the viewpoint, when it comes to establishing security and protecting the rule of law?
3. According to the viewpoint, how should Haiti's foreign debt be handled?

Two weeks after the earthquake that devastated Haiti [in January 2010], its people are confronted with a human rights crisis. Amnesty International has identified some of the

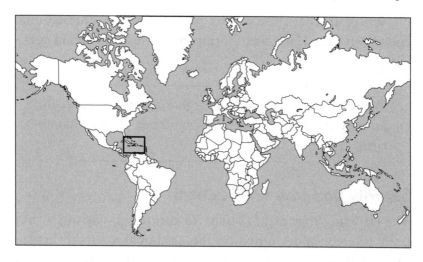

country's biggest human rights challenges and outlined a plan that puts protection of human rights at the core of relief and reconstruction efforts.

The Exploitation of Children

With families separated and schools destroyed, thousands of children in Haiti have been left without protection. The most vulnerable could become prey to the traffickers.

There is also a risk that children could be caught in irregular adoption processes—a risk increased by the interest of families abroad who would like to adopt Haitian children orphaned by the earthquake. Haitian institutions also have a lack of capacity to determine the status of children and ensure their rights are protected. Separated and unaccompanied children might wrongly be considered orphans.

International adoption should be a last resort, used only after domestic alternatives have been exhausted. The Haitian authorities must ensure children are not taken out of the country without the completion of formal legal proceedings for international adoption.

Family tracing should be a priority for the international community, the Haitian authorities and international aid agencies.

Two weeks after the earthquake that devastated Haiti [in January 2010], its people are confronted with a human rights crisis.

Security and Law Enforcement

The Haitian government's ability to ensure the rule of law has been severely undermined by the earthquake. Establishing a functional justice system to deal with the most serious crimes should be a top priority.

There is a growing concern that prisoners convicted of violent crimes who escaped from Port-au-Prince's National Penitentiary are trying to regain control of the most deprived and vulnerable communities.

In response to this threat, community members have organized themselves to prevent gangs from taking over communities. However, this could put community members at risk of spiralling violence. Amnesty International has received reports of lynchings and incidents of mob justice where alleged looters have been killed.

There are also reports of alleged looters being shot by police. Haitian authorities must ensure that firearms are only to be used by police in self-defence and as a last resort. The Haitian authorities must also set up a provisional detention centre, as the country's main prison has been destroyed and other detention centres are overcrowded.

Rights of the Displaced and Violence Against Women

Hundreds of thousands of people have been left homeless by the earthquake and many have fled the devastated areas.

"Donate to the poorest of the poor . . . Haitian relief," cartoon by Harley Schwadron, CartoonStock.com. Copyright © Harley Schwadron. Reproduction rights available from www.CartoonStock.com.

Displaced people must be supported to make voluntary and informed decisions about their future. Any relocation of internally displaced persons from camps or disaster areas must be voluntary, unless the safety and health of those affected require evacuation. They should not be coerced in any way, including through the suspension of assistance. All displaced persons have the right to return to their former homes unless safety issues prevent it.

In post-disaster situations, women and girls are often particularly at risk from sexual violence, exploitation by traffickers and reduced access to sexual, reproductive and maternal health services. Their disadvantage in accessing aid is well documented.

Those involved in the relief and reconstruction efforts must ensure that the prevention of all gender-based violence, in particular sexual violence, is integrated into their work.

Accountability of International Forces

More than 10,000 US troops, 150 military personnel from the Dominican Republic and 800 Canadian soldiers have been deployed in Haiti to provide security for the distribution of aid.

The terms of deployment and rules of engagement must be clarified from the onset and respected by all international forces. The United Nations [UN] Stabilization Mission in Haiti (MINUSTAH) personnel must also be governed by strict rules of accountability. In the past, leaving accountability for violations solely to the discretion of troop-contributing countries to UN peacekeeping missions has lead to impunity for serious human rights abuses.

In 2009, international financial institutions and other creditors cancelled US$1.2 billion of Haiti's foreign debt. Despite this, Haiti still owes hundreds of millions of dollars to its creditors.

The repayment of this debt now represents an unacceptable burden on Haiti's population and national economy. Amnesty International has called on all creditors to cancel Haiti's debt. Insistence on repayment would hinder Haiti's ability to meet its human rights obligations.

All financial resources available to Haiti in the years to come must be channelled to reconstruction programmes that ensure Haitians' welfare and access to basic services, and equitable and sustainable development.

Periodical and Internet Sources Bibliography

The following articles have been selected to supplement the diverse views presented in this chapter.

Morenike Akerele	"Between Honour Killings, Child Brides and Forced Marriages," *This Day* (Nigeria), October 12, 2010. http://allafrica.com.
Ali el-Bahnasawy	"Smoldering Lead," *Egypt Today*, March 2010.
Kathy Bushkin Calvin and Maria Eitel	"Poverty Stricken Adolescent Girls Can Become a Force for Change," Newsroom Panama, July 18, 2010.
Kanchan Chaudhari	"Victims Afraid to Report Cases: Survey," *Hindustan Times*, October 4, 2010.
Peter Goodspeed	"Analysis: Flotilla Violence Rips Open Political Wounds," *National Post* (Canada), June 2, 2010.
Godwin Haruna	"Curbing Female Genital Cutting," *This Day* (Nigeria), September 9, 2010. http://allafrica.com.
John McManus	"Is Caste Prejudice Still an Issue?" BBC News, June 8, 2009.
Trevor Phillips	"The Way to a Fairer Britain," *Guardian* (UK), October 11, 2010.
Navi Pillay	"We Must Stop Trading Off Women's Rights," *New Vision* (Uganda), September 23, 2010. http://allafrica.com.
Jack Shenker	"Tackling Sexual Harassment in Egypt," *Guardian* (UK), September 21, 2010.
Patricia Thangaraj	"Minister Byer-Suckoo Appeals for Accountability," *Barbados Advocate*, October 12, 2010.

For Further Discussion

Chapter 1

1. After reading the opening viewpoint by Amnesty International, what is your assessment on the global state of human rights? Were you surprised by Amnesty International's report, or encouraged? Why?

2. Do you agree or disagree with China's assessment of the state of human rights in the United States? What are China's reasons for releasing such a report?

Chapter 2

1. After reading the viewpoints in this chapter, list some of the ways politics can interfere with or hinder the quest for human rights in many countries. Which of these political methods do you think is the most destructive?

Chapter 3

1. The first viewpoint in the chapter focuses on caste-based discrimination. What is it, and where is it prevalent? How can it be eliminated?

2. In this chapter, all of the viewpoints examine how minority populations are oppressed by majorities. Describe what forms such discrimination can take. How can governments address such oppression?

Chapter 4

1. The fifth viewpoint of the chapter examines the challenges Haiti faces after the devastating earthquake it suffered in 2010. Which of these challenges do you think is the most pressing? Which solution would make the most difference?

2. This chapter enumerates the many human rights challenges the world faces. Of these, which do you think is the most difficult to address? How do you suggest governments and international organizations tackle this challenge?

Organizations to Contact

The editors have compiled the following list of organizations concerned with the issues debated in this book. The descriptions are derived from materials provided by the organizations. All have publications or information available for interested readers. The list was compiled on the date of publication of the present volume; the information provided here may change. Be aware that many organizations take several weeks or longer to respond to inquiries, so allow as much time as possible.

Amnesty International (AI)
1 Easton Street, London   WC1X 0DW
  United Kingdom
+44 20 741 35500 • fax: +44 20 795 61157
website: www.amnesty.org

Established in 1961, Amnesty International (AI) is one of the premier independent human rights organizations in the world. AI is made up of 2.8 million members, supporters, and activists who work together to address human rights abuses in more than 150 countries and territories. AI members and activists mobilize letter-writing campaigns, mass demonstrations, vigils, and direct lobbying efforts on behalf of individuals and groups being oppressed, tortured, and imprisoned for political, economic, social, or cultural reasons. Every year AI publishes the influential *State of the World's Human Rights* report, which assesses the global state of human rights. It also publishes monthly e-newsletters, *Stop Violence Against Women* and *Counter Terror with Justice*.

Center for Economic and Social Rights (CESR)
162 Montague Street, 3rd Floor, Brooklyn, NY   11201
(718) 237-9145 • fax: (718) 237-9147
e-mail: rights@cesr.org
website: www.cesr.org

The Center for Economic and Social Rights (CESR) is an international organization that promotes social justice through human rights. CESR describes its mission as such: "In a world where poverty and inequality deprive entire communities of dignity, justice, and sometimes life, we seek to uphold the universal human rights of every human being to education, health, food, water, housing, work, and other economic, social, and cultural rights essential to human dignity." In recent years, it has been developing new ways to measure and monitor economic and social rights compliance. The CESR website features a blog examining current human rights issues and CESR events. It also provides country fact sheets, in-depth studies on social rights issues, and other resources.

Equality Now
PO Box 20646, Columbus Circle Station
New York, NY   10023
(212) 586-1611
e-mail: info@equalitynow.org
website: www.equalitynow.org

Equality Now is an advocacy organization that works to protect and promote the human rights of women around the world. It documents violence and discrimination against women in a variety of contexts and coordinates with other human rights groups and activists to address these abuses. One of the organization's most important missions is to bring international attention to the issue. Equality Now is working on several campaigns such as opposition to female genital mutilation (FGM), eliminating sex trafficking, and politically and economically empowering women. On the Equality Now website, readers have access to press releases, press clips, and fact sheets on current campaigns.

Human Rights First
222 Seventh Avenue, 13th Floor, New York, NY   10001
(212) 845-5200 • fax: (212) 845-5299
e-mail: feedback@humanrightsfirst.org
website: www.humanrightsfirst.org

Human Rights First is an independent international human rights organization that advances human rights through accurate research and reporting on human rights abuses worldwide, advocacy for victims, and coordination with other human rights organizations. The group is focused in five key areas: crimes against humanity, fighting discrimination, aiding human rights activists, refugee protection, and advocating for fair legal protections. To that end, Human Rights First offers a series of in-depth studies on such issues, including recent reports on anti-Semitism in Europe, oppressive government counterterrorist measures in Uzbekistan, and China's role in the Sudanese conflict. It also provides an e-newsletter, *Rights Wire*, which examines topical issues in the human rights field.

Human Rights Foundation (HRF)

350 Fifth Avenue, #4515, New York, NY   10118
(212) 246-8486 • fax: (212) 643-4278
e-mail: info@thehrf.org
website: www.humanrightsfoundation.org

The Human Rights Foundation (HRF) is an independent human rights organization that is dedicated to protecting freedom of expression and self-determination in North, Central, and South America. The HRF creates programs that "provide education about what constitutes a free society, why freedom matters, and how freedom is nurtured, developed, and sustained." Another mission of the organization is to report on human rights abuses, particularly on cases of political prisoners and prisoners of conscience. Several of these in-depth alerts and reports can be accessed on the HRF's website.

Human Rights Watch (HRW)

350 Fifth Avenue, 34th Floor, New York, NY   10118
(212) 290-4700 • fax: (212) 736-1300
e-mail: hrwpress@hrw.org
website: www.hrw.org

Founded in 1978, Human Rights Watch (HRW) is a non-profit, independent human rights group that researches and publishes more than one hundred reports to shed light on pressing human rights abuses. Often working in difficult situations—including oppressive and tyrannical governments—the HRW strives to provide accurate and impartial reporting on human rights conditions for the media, financial institutions, and international organizations. The group's wide-ranging and thorough reports can be accessed on the HRW' website. Interested viewers can also access video, audio, podcasts, photo-essays, and photo galleries.

Institute on Religion and Public Policy

500 North Washington Street, Alexandria, VA   22314
(703) 888-1700 • fax: (703) 888-1704
website: http://religionandpolicy.org

The Institute on Religion and Public Policy is an international, nonpartisan organization that works to protect the practice of religious freedom around the world. To that end, it researches and disseminates information and analysis on oppressive governments and policies that threaten that freedom. The institute also sponsors programs and events to educate and motivate activists, government policy makers, academics, business executives, religious leaders, and nongovernmental organizations. It publishes a weekly newsletter, *Face of Freedom*, which offers analysis on the state of global religious freedom. In addition, the institute's website also features a blog focusing on current issues and events.

International Alliance for Women (TIAW)

48 Coledale Road, Markham, Ontario   L3R 7W9
   Canada
(905) 948-1994 • fax: (905) 305-1548
e-mail: info@TIAW.org
website: www.tiaw.org

The International Alliance for Women (TIAW) is a nonprofit organization formed to advance the cause of working women around the world. Established in 1980, TIAW is dedicated to empowering women economically and politically. One of the ways it fulfills its goal is to organize events that bring a diverse group of working women together to foster greater understanding and opportunities; these events include conferences, seminars, networking meetings, and lectures. Another way it advances the cause of working women is through a number of programs: the Microenterprise Development Program, which facilitates microloans to impoverished women in developing countries to start businesses; an Entrepreneurship program, focusing on education; and a Corporate Women's Leadership Network program. It also publishes *eConnections*, a newsletter that examines subjects of interest to members.

International Federation for Human Rights (FIDH)

17, passage de la main d'or, Paris   75011
   France
+33 143 55 25 18 • fax: +33 143 55 18 80
website: www.fidh.org

The International Federation for Human Rights (FIDH) aims to prevent human rights abuses and encourage the prosecution of those who manage to perpetrate them. On its website, it describes its mission as follows: "In these times of paradox and uncertainty for human rights, FIDH aims to embody a renewed ambition: to successfully complete its transformation from a credible and recognised INGO (international nongovernmental organization) into a strong universal movement for the effectiveness of universal human rights: a unique gathering of actors from the field capable of influencing in a unique manner the course of events leading to tragedy, preventing the perpetration of international crimes, and consolidating the indivisible paths of peace, democracy and development." The FIDH's website features videos, a blog, and information on recent human rights campaigns.

International Gay and Lesbian Human Rights Commission (IGLHRC)

80 Maiden Lane, Suite 1505, New York, NY   10038

(212) 430-6054 • fax: (212) 430-6060
e-mail: iglhrc@iglhrc.org
website: www.iglhrc.org

The International Gay and Lesbian Human Rights Commission (IGLHRC) is an independent international organization working to advance the human rights protection of gays and lesbians and others discriminated against because of their actual or perceived sexual orientation, gender identity, or gender expression. To this end, the IGLHRC builds advocacy partnerships with local activists to address pressing human rights issues and strengthen local human rights frameworks. It also works to connect local and regional activists with international organizations such as the United Nations and nongovernmental organizations. The IGLHRC publishes a series of reports on the state of human rights in a number of countries, annual reports, the *Outspoken* newsletter, and training materials.

International Partnership for Human Rights (IPHR)
Blvd. Bischoffsheim 11, 8th Floor, Brussels   1000
   Belgium
+32 475 39 2121
e-mail: IPHR@IPHRonline.org
website: www.iphronline.org

The International Partnership for Human Rights (IPHR) is a nonprofit human rights organization made up of practitioners and activists dedicated to promoting human rights around the world. IPHR researches and reports on human rights abuses and governmental compliance with human rights obligations; coordinates policy on the issue with international organizations, nongovernmental groups, and local activists; and develops and implements projects that advance the global state of human rights. The IPHR website features access to various reports, studies, letters, press releases, and news articles on relevant topics.

Society for Threatened Peoples
PO Box 2024, D-37010 Göttingen, Geiststraße 7
Göttingen   D-37073
   Germany
+49-551-49906-0 • fax: +49-551-58028
e-mail: info@gfbv.de
website: www.gfbv.de

The Society for Threatened Peoples is an independent human rights group that vows to live by the motto: "Not turning a blind eye." With the help of individual members, the organization develops and implements human rights campaigns all over the world, such as putting an end to slavery in Mauritania; helping the Masai people to keep their land; and releasing Bahá'í prisoners in Iran. It also researches reports and studies on pressing human rights issues, such as the rights of indigenous peoples, the persecution of Uighurs, and the current situation in Burma. The Society for Threatened Peoples publishes the *GfbV* magazine, which provides updated information on recent campaigns.

United Nations Human Rights Council (HRC)
Palais des Nations, Geneva 10   CH-1211
   Switzerland
+41 22 917 9220
e-mail: InfoDesk@ohchr.org
website: www.ohchr.org

The Human Rights Council (HRC) is a part of the United Nations Office of the High Commissioner for Human Rights. It is made up of forty-seven member states that focus on strengthening and protecting human rights around the globe. The HRC is tasked with making recommendations on some of the most pressing human rights situations today. It works closely with other bodies in the United Nations as well as with national and local governments, nongovernmental organizations, and human rights activists. Transcripts and videos of the HRC's sessions can be found on the group's website, which also features current news and information on recent reports and proceedings.

Bibliography of Books

Adekeye Adebajo, ed. — *From Global Apartheid to Global Village: Africa and the United Nations.* Scottsville, South Africa: University of KwaZulu-Natal Press, 2009.

John Akokpari and Daniel Shea Zimbler, eds. — *Africa's Human Rights Architecture.* Auckland Park, South Africa: Fanele, 2008.

J. Kirk Boyd — *2048: Humanity's Agreement to Live Together.* San Francisco, CA: Berrett-Koehler, 2010.

Alice Bullard, ed. — *Human Rights in Crisis.* Aldershot, England: Ashgate, 2008.

Anthony Tirado Chase and Amr Hamzawy, eds. — *Human Rights in the Arab World: Independent Voices.* Philadelphia: University of Pennsylvania Press, 2006.

Kenneth Christie — *America's War on Terrorism: The Revival of the Nation-State Versus Universal Human Rights.* Lewiston, New York: Edwin Mellen Press, 2008.

Solomon A. Dersso, ed. — *Promotion of Human Security in Africa: The Role of African Human Rights Institutions.* Tshwane, South Africa: Institute for Security Studies, 2008.

Caroline Fleay — *Australia and Human Rights: Situating the Howard Government.* Newcastle upon Tyne, United Kingdom: Cambridge Scholars Publishers, 2010.

Rashmi Gupta

Tibetans in Exile: Struggle for Human Rights. New Delhi, India: Anamika Publishers, 2010.

Rhoda E. Howard-Hassmann

Can Globalization Promote Human Rights? University Park, PA: Pennsylvania State University Press, 2010.

Deena R. Hurwitz and Margaret L. Satterthwaite, eds.

Human Rights Advocacy Stories. New York: Foundation Press, 2009.

Ronald C. Keith and Zhiqiu Lin

New Crime in China: Public Order and Human Rights. London: Routledge, 2006.

David Kennedy

The Rights of Spring: A Memoir of Innocence Abroad. Princeton, NJ: Princeton University Press, 2009.

Ross Lambertson

Repression and Resistance: Canadian Human Rights Activists, 1930–1960. Toronto, ON: University of Toronto Press, 2005.

Rosanna L. Langer

Defining Rights and Wrongs: Bureaucracy, Human Rights, and Public Accountability. Vancouver, BC: UBC Press, 2007.

S. Neil MacFarlane and Yuen Foong Khong

Human Security and the UN: A Critical History. Bloomington: Indiana University Press, 2006.

D. Soyini Madison

Acts of Activism: Human Rights as Radical Performance. New York: Cambridge University Press, 2010.

Lee R. Massingdale, ed.	*Human Rights in China.* New York: Nova Science Publishers, 2009.
Bertrand G. Ramcharan	*Contemporary Human Rights Ideas.* New York: Routledge, 2008.
Alden T. Roycee, ed.	*Burma in Turmoil.* New York: Nova Science Publishers, 2008.
Cynthia Soohoo, Catherine Albisa, and Martha F. Davis, eds.	*Bringing Human Rights Home: A History of Human Rights in the United States.* Philadelphia: University of Pennsylvania Press, 2009.
Curtis Stokes, ed.	*Race and Human Rights.* East Lansing: Michigan State University Press, 2008.
Maxwell Yalden	*Transforming Rights: Reflections from the Front Lines.* Toronto, ON: University of Toronto Press, 2009.

Index

Geographic headings and page numbers in **boldface** refer to viewpoints about that country or region.